THE THOUSAND YEAR OLD GARDEN

INSIDE THE SECRET GARDEN AT LAMBETH PALACE

NICK STEWART SMITH

ILLUSTRATED BY ELLIE GIBSON

T0243495

For Gillian

*With special thanks to Kirsty McLachlan at Morgan
Green Creatives for her help and guidance with this book*

First published 2023

The History Press
97 St George's Place, Cheltenham,
Gloucestershire, GL50 3QB
www.thehistorypress.co.uk

British Library Cataloguing in Publication Data.
A catalogue record for this book is available from the British Library.

ISBN 978 1 80399 304 1

Typesetting and origination by The History Press
Printed and bound in Great Britain by TJ Books Limited, Padstow, Cornwall.

Trees for LYfe

CONTENTS

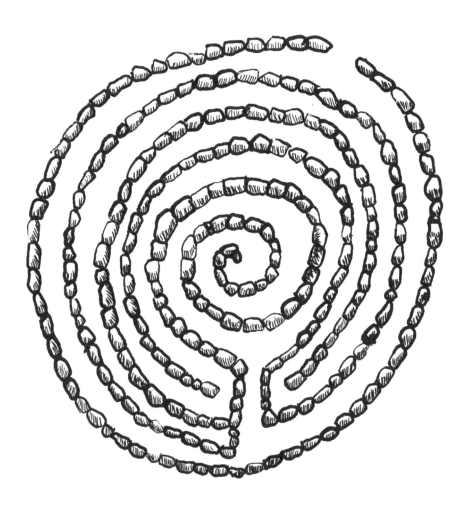

INTRODUCTION

Nearly all of my working life has been spent gardening. For ten years, I was a National Trust head gardener in Devon, moving to the Chequers Estate in the Chilterns for a further seven years, followed by another six looking after the Archbishop of Canterbury's historic garden at Lambeth Palace. At all these places, my time was spent outside among the plants. I hardly ever wrote anything down, nothing more than a page or two of notes, and it never occurred to me to try anything longer, let alone attempt to write a book.

Then, a little while ago, I gave a guided tour around the garden at Lambeth Palace for a couple named Claire and Seán. I must have given more than 500 guided garden tours over the years, but this one was somehow different and the warm autumn afternoon we spent together has stayed with me. There was an unusual energy in the air and the conversation seemed to flow easily from one unexpected observation to another without prompting.

The tour ended by a strawberry vine I had carefully trained on the rails by the herb garden, a new plant now heavy with small grapes that were sweet to taste. Any gardener is always inexplicably proud when something they have planted reaches the point of bearing fruit or flowering fully for the first time. So, I encouraged Claire and Seán to try the grapes before saying goodbye to them.

'You should write all this down,' said Claire, referring back to the tour.

'Ah, yes, well, I don't know ...' I mumbled in reply.

'No, you should. You should try,' she said.

A few days later, on arriving at Lambeth Palace, I found that Claire had left her most recent book for me, *Miles to go Before I Sleep: Letters on Hope, Death and Learning to Live* (Claire Gilbert, 2021). I read it over the next week and it made a deep impression on me, helping me in ways I could not have foreseen.

In my pigeon hole with the other post there was also a brand new notebook. I took this with me and began to write sentences on the pages, one word after another slowly growing into something much longer until all the pages were filled and I had the beginnings of this book.

Everything is strangely quiet this morning. It is seven o'clock and I am crossing the Walworth Road, usually a mass of cars and lorries with grunting engines coughing toxins into the spring air by this time of day. But now there is almost nothing here, just a red bus, empty of passengers, that pulls with a sigh to a stop where nobody is waiting.

I am making my way to Lambeth Palace, where I work as a gardener, around 3 miles from my home but an easy stroll through small parks and side streets. As I get nearer to the Thames, the traffic turns heavier with drivers anxious to progress but stuck at the lights in long queues. Exhaust fumes linger in the air but the trees lining the street have fresh, green leaves and they are giving off a sweet scent.

At the junction where the wide span of Lambeth Bridge appears, I see glimpses of the immense brown river flowing underneath. People are on the pavements even at this early hour, some of them might be tourists as they are carrying cameras and seem a little dazed, taking pictures of themselves standing in front of the palace's medieval brick towers, which look vast and powerful this morning.

I am a few minutes late, so I walk quickly towards those towers where there are two wooden doors, one big to allow vehicles to enter, the other much smaller for someone on foot, like me. Lambeth Palace is beyond the doors, workplace and home to the archbishops of Canterbury for more than 800 years. Surrounding the buildings are 10 acres of secluded gardens, which are even older than the palace, hidden away from view behind high brick walls through the centuries, hidden away from the noise and bustle of a changing London.

I knock on the door and hold my breath for a few seconds. The traffic rumbles by and then I hear the shuffle of footsteps on the other side as a security guard approaches. The door swings open and I walk in and cross the courtyard, then through a small stone arch where another world opens up before me, a secret garden filled with its own kind of sound and movement, its own light and colour.

LATE SPRING

ive olive trees were delivered towards the end of March. I had to go away for a short while and those trees made it through the gates just too late for me to do anything with them. So, they were left strapped close together, held captive on a narrow, wooden palette that I dragged behind the greenhouse. Earlier this morning, I could at last untie the trees, get them out and transfer them into bigger pots where they would have more light and a little more space to grow into. Those olive trees could breathe again.

The middle of London is a very long way from the dry, stony fields where they started as saplings in southern Spain, baking in the heat of the long Andalusian summers. Given the opportunity, and with a bit of luck, they might spend the rest of their lives in their new northern home; lives that could last several hundred years at least. I have nearly thirty of them now, beginning to form an avenue either side of the wide gravel path running behind Lambeth Palace.

With my wheelbarrow, I am walking down that path between the lines of olive trees. A small group of NHS staff are gathered around one of the old benches there, all dressed in their uniforms. St Thomas' Hospital next door has been given a spare key to the garden's back gate so that the staff can come and go from over the road as and when they wish, even if that is only for half an hour to get some rest, to find some peace for a brief time in the quiet green surroundings.

The air might be cold today but the sky is a brilliant blue above with some shade provided by the new leaves unfurling on the trees, and there is birdsong all around. It feels like a good place to be. They can sit there on the old oak bench with the rest of the world at a distance, there is no need even to speak. Hopefully, the working day moves a little further away, at least for a while, giving some time and space to prepare again for whatever is to come.

With the sun rising higher, I leave my barrow to move further down the gravel path and onto the grass. Like most mornings recently, this one will be spent watering the many terracotta pots and oak barrels placed around the garden, as well as giving a little water to all the things that were planted in the early spring. Everything is so dry now that I can feel the parched ground as hard as rocks under my feet when I move across the lawn.

Despite the difficult weather, I can see a lot of the incidental plants are doing well; they include foxgloves, wild gladiolus and nigellas in various shades of blue. All seem to have flowered a little earlier than might have been expected. These self-seeders are like nomads wandering through, stopping at different areas of the garden each year, where they show off their flowers, display their colours and maybe reveal their scents before they pack up for the season, turning up somewhere else next time. They can catch anyone unawares, which does not seem such a bad thing, appearing as they do unexpectedly where there is just a little dapple of shade, a little water, somewhere to pause and flourish, if only for a brief time, before moving on, always moving on.

Their seeds ripened last autumn as the rest of the plant died. Some seeds are no more than fine dust floating on the air, unsure where they will land. But when they do – and the situation suits – little root tendrils are sent down to explore the dark soil, hurrying to begin new life before everything else can crowd the space and close the light. This year, there has been a good germination and the garden is full of those early flowers: snapdragons, larkspur, purple toadflax and all the others. It's like a dream.

As these self-seeding, nomadic, wild things drift through the space, they provide a kind of bridge for the garden between the late spring and the true beginning of summer. There is usually a natural pause in flowering just then, those few weeks when the early blooms are over and before the perennials get going in all their glory come June.

It is never easy to find a balance gardening this way, to decide which chance seedlings are wanted and which, perhaps, are not. I intervene now and then, and the decisions I make will change from year to year. But there is not too much intervention; I shouldn't forget to just allow things to happen around me and give those wandering plants some room to roam. I let them choose for themselves where they are going to go – which might not be where I had been thinking they ought to go. It becomes a back and forth, a conversation. The garden is allowed to speak and it's not just you or I trying to impose our will on it. Instead, another voice is present. I think gardens are always speaking to anyone who cares to pay attention.

Of those self-seeding plants I have been looking at, foxglove and larkspur are described as North European natives. Some of the others, the gladiolus, the snapdragon and the purple toadflax, have their origins in Mediterranean areas, while nigella comes from further away, from eastern Europe and Asia, although now it is widely naturalised across much of the world.

The fascination with non-native plants has been a part of gardening in most places for hundreds of years, a fascination with the strange and the exotic. But there should still be space for the indigenous plants. For example, if the lawn I am standing on were allowed to grow a bit longer, especially now, in late spring, some of the suppressed native plants could come through. Plants such as cat's ear, yarrow or knapweed would have a chance to flower, along with the daisies, buttercups and speedwell, providing much to attract many kinds of insects. Relaxing the mowing in this way across thousands of gardens could make quite a difference when put together, creating huge swathes of rich habitat, with lawns no longer a monotonous, even green but instead scattered with tiny flowers like jewels, the grass studded with colour and scent.

I have walked across the hard surface of the grass and up the short flight of stone steps to a raised terrace that cuts across the middle of the garden. Spring bulbs are flowering everywhere, including the more recent additions of orange tulips and deep blue muscari. When the rains come in the autumn and the days turn colder, I might be found hidden away in the shed being tempted by the descriptions in catalogues for various bulbs and seeds, wondering what new things to get, calculating how much I can afford. I keep my eye on the native selections as I try to find a balance with those plants from faraway lands that have been so attractive to me for so long.

Next year, I could increase the numbers of snowdrops, wood anemones and snake's head fritillaries, wild daffodils too. Maybe not all natives, by definition, but at least with a centuries-long history in the north European landscape.

As I add new things, I am trying to observe and survey in more detail what is already present in the garden, creatures as well as plants, and to write it down each day in a notebook. And if that could be done through the years, I could build a picture of the changes that are taking place with the wildlife in the green space around me.

It is still spring but it feels as if summer is already somewhere nearby and there is a lot going on. The roses are just beginning, they are going to have a good year with hundreds of flowers already in bud. The air sings in anticipation and I detect a faint perfume, although no blooms have opened yet. Alliums are also making their presence felt with delicate globes in different shades of purple floating above the borders, while blood-red astrantias can be seen here and there, along with many chance columbine seedlings.

The iris are also looking good at the moment, from soft white to pale blue to rich purple, with some newer ones of copper orange. These plants are named for the goddess Iris, who carries messages from the earth to the heavens by ascending on the arc of a rainbow, her bridge, and in that way allowing the living to send messages to the dead in the worlds beyond. In modern Greece, purple iris are still planted on the graves of women to summon the goddess, so that she can guide their souls from this world to the next.

The hours go quickly by and, too soon, the day is nearly over, although neither the watering nor the weeding are quite finished. The hospital staff left their resting place around the oak bench ages ago but I didn't see them leave. I expect a group of them will return again tomorrow. For me, only an hour or so remains and there is so much to be done – but not enough time, never enough time.

The spring breeze picks up from the west and I hear the faint sound of last year's leftover dead leaves stirring in the hidden corners of the garden. I will leave them in peace. I know that down in the decaying brown of those leaves there are safe places for all kinds of creatures to make a life. I will leave some of the twigs and branches that have fallen from the trees, make neat stacks of them so that they can rot away in their own time, crumbling to provide a whole world of possibilities for bugs and other wildlife.

Pausing for a short while in the shelter of the herb garden, I am looking at the torn electric cable that used to carry the power to the pump in the small round pond. There is no mistaking those teethmarks, something has bitten right through the wires – foxes, on their nightly patrols around here, no doubt. They sense movement in these types of cables, tiny vibrations, and they attack in the hope of finding something alive and interesting inside. All they could have got for their efforts with that particular cable would have been a sudden slight shock as they crouched there in the shadows to chew through the black casing, exposing the electric current while, in the night garden around them, the dark waves of aromatic herbs would sway softly in the moonlight.

With the cable broken, the pump has been disabled and this has allowed a layer of green blanket weed to cover the pond surface. The fox sabotage gives me a reminder that the electric pump should have been replaced long ago with a pump powered by a small solar panel. I will get to that soon. But in the meantime, there is a lot of green weed to be cleared.

Looking closer, I find the dense living blanket is inhabited by dozens of little smooth newts, and it takes quite a while to free each of them. Some lie still in my hand for a few moments, as if playing dead, then struggle furiously as soon as they sense the chance to escape and disappear at speed down into the safe depths of the pond where it is dark. One I was untangling from the blanket weed even covered its face with its front limbs, finger digits all splayed, eyes shut tight, maybe hoping in that way not to be seen. After all, if I can't see you, then surely you can't see me. Or can you?

Those juvenile newts will crawl out of the water as the summer reaches an end and their gills are gone. They will find somewhere to shelter in the undergrowth of the surrounding planting before returning to the pond to breed as the weather warms up again the following year. I leave them to it, walking away with the gravel path crunching quietly beneath my feet. The sky has become overcast, layer on layer of low cloud, grey on grey. I think it might rain after all.

THE BLAKES OF LAMBETH

A punctured bike tyre and no repair kit means I have to go to work on foot again today. I leave the apartment block in the early morning and start walking along Blake's Road, where I live. It is usually a quiet street. At this hour, just before sunrise, nobody is around. The spring is still here and there is even a little ice on the pavement as a reminder that winter has not quite gone. The various cars lined up by the kerb all have frosted windshields. We are in the north part of the borough, traditionally known as one of the rougher parts of Peckham, although it doesn't seem so bad today, especially with the first rays of morning sun piercing the luminous grey sky.

The street where I live is named for William Blake, due to his childhood associations with the area. His habit from around the age of 7 was to take long solitary walks far from his family home in Soho, and on some occasions, he even walked the 6 miles in a southerly direction to get to one of his favourite places, the big green common at Peckham Rye. That open space is still there, much appreciated by the locals and not far from where I am now.

More than 250 years after young William Blake passed this way, when the apartment block where I live was built, the builders chose to name it Blake's Apartments in a kind of tribute to the poet, I suppose. It is a nice enough building, a conventional low-rise residential block of the twenty-first-century style, finished in the same way as many of the other buildings in the area. Of course, there is no knowing what William Blake might have made of all this – a modern block of flats named after him – but if he had anything to say, it would be something surprising, I imagine.

Walking from Soho to Peckham Rye would have taken him a couple of hours at least. It is a long way for such a young boy to go for a stroll all alone, stepping out into a world where any number of things could have happened. One day, on reaching the Rye, he looked up into one of the trees and saw that it was filled with angels. He saw their bejewelled wings outspread among the branches, spangled and sparkling as if covered with stars made of fire.

Some twenty-five years after that spectacular childhood vision, by then still largely unknown in his calling as an artist and poet, he moved with his wife Catherine into a small house in north Lambeth at No. 13 Hercules Road. They lived there from 1790 to 1800, their top floor overlooking the grounds and gardens of Lambeth Palace, which in those days extended much further than now, nearly double the present size, so that the garden walls would have been on the other side of the Blakes' new street.

In that house in Hercules Road, the two of them imagined and produced much of the work that is still admired all around the world more than 200 years later, including the finished versions of *Songs of Innocence and Experience*, which they self-published in 1794. Imagery is woven through those songs that involves gardens, trees and especially flowers – their species, shapes and colours are always of key significance. The engraving on page 43 of the 1794 edition of *Songs of Experience* has three of the works most strongly inspired by the language of flowers, 'My Pretty Rose Tree', 'Ah! Sun-flower' and 'The Lily'. For me, as a gardener at Lambeth Palace, it is curious to reflect that the extraordinary flower imagery of these works was produced while the Blakes were living alongside the 20 acres of the palace gardens.

Catherine and William Blake had a garden of their own adjoining their Lambeth home and it is recorded that they planted a fig tree and grape vine, among several other things. The now world-famous Lambeth Palace fig tree in the garden opposite would already have been nearly 250 years old by then. It must have been of a considerable size and well known in the local area. It is possible that the Blakes' fig tree was a cutting from their neighbour's vast garden. Back then, I don't know if one of them could have simply knocked at Lambeth Palace's forbidding entranceway and asked for a cutting or two. Perhaps those gates were always kept shut tight with 'Thou shalt not' carved into stone over the archway.

It seems unlikely that they would have obtained a fig cutting in those days just by asking at the front door. I wonder if they could have befriended one or two of the gardeners at the palace. They lived so close by, right next to each other, for ten years after all, so it is possible the Blakes were given a small fig tree in secret by one of their gardener friends; something special, quietly handed over the high wall as the rosy dawn was filling the sky above Hercules Road. Catherine Blake's father was a gardener by profession and she might have known very well how to deal with cuttings and plants of most kinds, including fig trees. With the skills and knowledge gained from growing up in a home where gardening was the main source of income, I think it is possible that she could have guided the planting of the Blakes' Lambeth garden.

With William often occupied in the rich and strange worlds of his extraordinary imagination, it fell to Catherine to take charge and manage the couple's often fragile finances. She was also closely involved practically with the many artworks they created; her significant contributions were not fully acknowledged at the time, nor over the subsequent years. She mixed the colours used in the paintings and illustrations, carrying out some of the colouring herself, while also becoming a skilled engraver and printmaker, essential for the production of the beautiful books they assembled at home. Her role in the work was active and essential, it was a two-person venture.

Their marriage was very close and lasted for forty-five years, until William's death in 1827. Catherine lived for another three years, managing on small loans and help from friends as well as by selling some of the paintings she and William had made. Neither of them had much recognition for their work in their lifetimes, one telling example being the only review of William's self-funded 1809 exhibition in Golden Square, which stated, 'The poor man fancies himself a great master and has painted a few wretched pictures.' The show itself was very sparsely attended and that review may have been the only one in print the Blakes received while William was alive.

Among the precious objects the Blakes produced while living in Lambeth for those ten years is a hand-finished relief etching titled *God Judging Adam*, dated 1795. The composition shows two powerful figures, physically mirroring each other, as it should be, for we are told that Adam was created in God's own image. The Bible also tells that Adam was the First Man and was shaped from clay and soil.

The two figures in the etching may look the same but their stances are very different. Adam is strong and muscled but his head hangs low in despair, his long grey hair drooping around his face, while the figure of God is opposite, seated above Adam among bright flames in a chariot made of fire and pulled by horses with manes made from flame. There is a book open on God's knees, although no writing is visible.

The Blakes' composition is dominated by the dynamic diagonal line of God's arm and long index finger, sending what appears to be a white beam of light through the top of Adam's bowed head by way of punishment or maybe illumination, possibly both. The expression on the face of the figure depicting God is difficult to read. I have looked at the face for a long time and would not describe it as an expression of wrath or anger, although definitely something is there. The feeling is more a mixture of sorrow and disappointment, almost resignation, as if knowing that this was always the way things would turn out.

Made from the clay of the ground, Adam, the First Man, has also sometimes been referred to as the first gardener: 'Now the Lord God planted a garden in the east, in Eden, and there he put the man he had formed ... and put him in the Garden of Eden to tend and to keep it' (Genesis 2:8). In the picture I have in my mind, I see Adam on his knees working in that garden, a small figure surrounded by the wonders of the immense green world so full of life all around him.

The painting *God Judging Adam* is to be found these days as part of the Metropolitan Museum's collection in New York. More than 200 years after it was completed in Hercules Road, the picture is now a prized treasure in a renowned museum on the other side of the Atlantic Ocean, some 3,500 miles away from Lambeth. Considering it was once among artworks that were described as 'wretched' in their own time, a place in the Metropolitan Museum's collection does not seem too bad.

William and Catherine Blake endured the hardships and seemed to shrug off the unkind jibes that came their way as best they could. They carried on, somehow never losing their faith in what they were doing, the two of them together, maybe not having very much but getting by with hope as their currency. It is reported that the combined version of *Songs of Innocence and Experience* had sold fewer than thirty copies by the time of William's death – fewer than thirty copies sold in over thirty years. Now it is believed there are twenty-eight copies of the original printing still in existence, all individual with unique variations. Although most are carefully preserved in libraries and museums around the world, one or two still remain in private collections. Imagine glancing at the bookshelf at home and seeing a hand-finished original copy of *Songs of Innocence and Experience* just waiting to be taken down and opened.

As I venture out into the garden today, the storm clouds are gathering above and the sky looks a metallic grey but ready to dissolve at any moment. Standing here with eyes uplifted, I'm still thinking about the Lambeth Palace gardener at the top of a ladder handing a fig tree cutting over the high wall to the Blakes, who are waiting on the other side as arranged. It would have been early in the morning, with the air quite cold, a thin layer of crystal frost covering the ground as the little tree in its terracotta pot is safely exchanged; a precious thing handed over the wall from one gardener to another.

More than 200 years later, I am still wondering about all of that while walking back along Blake's Road in Peckham on a spring evening, slowly home to Blake's Apartments. There are no angels in the trees, there are no stars of fire up there among the branches, at least none that I can see. Maybe next time – you never know.

To see Eternity in a Grain of Sand
And a Heaven in a Wild Flower
Hold Infinity in the palm of your hand
And Eternity in an Hour

From 'Auguries of Innocence' by William Blake, 1803.

BY THE FIG AND THE OLIVE

Yesterday, a message was received in the garden office. It came from Sergeant Major Saheed Khan, who is stationed at Sandhurst, and described a recent visit to Lambeth Palace. He wrote that he was especially impressed by the ancient fig tree in the main courtyard and wondered if he could have a couple of cuttings to grow, with the idea of eventually planting a new tree outside the mosque in Redditch, his hometown. There, it would act as a living symbol, he wrote, to show the 'unity, tolerance and good relations between Muslim and Christian'.

For many centuries, gardening has played a significant role in Muslim tradition and culture, with the gardens of Islam being some of the finest ever created anywhere. They contained plots for growing useful plants – those that would provide medicine, food and other practical materials. But their gardens were also held to be something more. They were places for relaxation and pleasure, valued as secluded and peaceful places with quiet areas for thought and contemplation. Usually, a small pond would be found at the centre with channels of water running to it from the corners of the enclosed area. The water was to provide gentle sound and movement, while the high walls surrounding the garden were to provide shelter and protection. Neat paths would be laid out just inside the wall perimeter, encouraging the full use of the space as a whole.

A large-scale example of such an Islamic paradise garden can be found in Granada, southern Spain, where the Generalife forms part of the magnificent Alhambra complex, the construction of which began around the same time that the first Lambeth Palace was being completed in London.

My last visit to the Generalife was quite a few years ago on a winter day. It was very cold, cold enough for snow to begin to fall. I was standing looking up at the snow fluttering down, having travelled a long way south to where the sun nearly always shines – unbroken sunshine every day, or at least, that's what I heard. Nobody was around, but for some reason a small covered stall had remained open, selling hot coffee and small cakes. I approached cautiously through the white flurry to speak to the elderly woman, who was warmly wrapped up behind the wooden counter.

'Is this normal, all this snow?' I asked.

'It isn't normal, but it happens sometimes,' she answered.

'Every year?'

'Not every year, last time was in 1962.'

'Really? 1962?'

'Well, it could have been 1961. I don't remember exactly,' she said with a smile.

The coffee was strong and sweet and warmed my hands as I wandered slowly through the deserted courtyards, stopping here and there to sit on a stone bench or pausing to consider the views of the winter hillsides framed by openings carefully carved in the stone walls. At the far end of the gardens there is a flight of stairs with handrails like no others I have ever seen. They are long and wriggle upwards in a serpentine design with a narrow channel of water flowing down the middle of each, like a liquid banister. Looking closely at the clay from which these handrails are made, it is possible to make out various impressions made by fingerprints. I don't know if these are originals going back centuries or were left there by workers making repairs in more modern times. Nevertheless, on that winter day, I placed my own thumb on the clay print of a thumb in the water handrail and, in this way, could imagine I was making contact with a Muslim gardener from all those centuries ago. Meanwhile, the snow kept falling in the empty courtyards.

Today I am sitting here in London, nearly 1,500 miles away from the Alhambra, still in the garden office at Lambeth Palace and looking again at the letter from Sergeant Major Khan. I am wondering if he has a garden of his own and what that might be like. I am thinking how a fig tree growing outside the Redditch Mosque would look. It should be a marvellous sight in years to come. Hopefully, he will be able to visit later on in the year and then I can give him a few branches from the tree itself, ideally in December after the leaves have fallen and the fig is at a quiet stage and fairly dormant, with the milky sap no longer rising. To cut during the growing season would cause excessive bleeding of that sap and the bleeding can seriously weaken the tree. I will try to have a surprise ready for Sergeant Major Khan – an already prepared rooted cutting that he can take away with him as well, if he wishes to.

The best way to make these cuttings is to follow the natural inclinations of the tree itself. As the branches get heavier with age, they tend to slowly lower themselves down towards the ground, as if to rest there and lean those big wooden elbows on the earth for a while to take a breather. Where the bark comes into contact with the soil, new roots often begin to form, creating a new access point for the tree to draw up water and dissolved nutrients from the ground. Gardeners can speed up this process by bending a flexible stem near the base and fastening it to the ground with a metal pin of some kind; a strong tent peg or a croquet hoop would do. This allows those new roots to be created and get a hold where contact is made between the pinned stem and the soil without having to wait for the tree to rest a branch on the ground by itself. After at least a year or so, at an opportune moment in the winter, careful cuts have to be made to that pinned branch either side of the point of contact with the earth. Then the newly rooted cutting can be dug up and separated from the parent tree, ready to begin a new life somewhere else. This method of propagation is known as layering.

In February, earlier this year, we gave Sir David Attenborough a small fig tree in a clay pot as a gift, a cutting that was maybe two or three years old, having been propagated by a layering from the original tree. I wonder how it is getting on in his garden. Flourishing, I would imagine, under his care.

Fig trees appear in various sacred texts, including several passages of the Bible. In Genesis 3:7, Adam and Eve are described as fashioning garments for themselves by sewing fig leaves together to hide the feelings of shame caused by their nakedness, which had been revealed to them after they had eaten forbidden fruit from the Tree of Knowledge. That particular tree is often thought to have been an apple, although some scholars have concluded that it could have been a fig.

Between 1508 and 1512, Michelangelo was working on the ceiling of the Sistine Chapel at the Vatican, with nine scenes from the Book of Genesis central to the composition of his painting. His back was giving him terrible pain as he crouched high on the painter's scaffold that had been set up for him, describing himself as contorted up there 'like a cat from Lombardy'. When depicting the temptation and subsequent expulsion of Adam and Eve from Eden, he showed the Tree of Knowledge not as an apple but as a fig, possibly modelling it on one of the plants he had seen in the luxurious gardens surrounding the Vatican.

Some forty years after the Sistine Chapel ceiling was completed, in the summer of 1556, the sitting Archbishop of Canterbury, Cardinal Pole visited the Pope and brought back to Lambeth Palace some small fig trees that were part of the various gifts received while in Rome. Maybe they were cuttings from trees growing in the Vatican garden, maybe even from the very same tree that had served as a model for Michelangelo. Whatever the case, it must have been a quite a journey for those fig cuttings, all the way from Rome to London over miles and miles of rugged countryside, bumping along in a horse-drawn cart eventually to cross the sea by ship, until the mouth of the Thames was at last sighted. Then those plants and the rest of the cargo would have come up the brown river for several more miles in a barge until, with some relief, the worn-out crew reached the familiar jetty at Lambeth Palace.

After the long and tiring trip, I expect the tree cuttings might have been overlooked as one of the least important items of luggage.

Perhaps they were noticed at the last minute as the sun was sinking behind the Palace of Westminster on the opposite bank. Perhaps those plants were carelessly swept up and thrust by one of Archbishop Pole's weary servants in the general direction of the gardener, who happened to be standing by, lingering there at the riverside, just in case. 'Do something with these, good sir!' might have been yelled, or probably something much saltier.

As the golden light faded and dusk settled in, the resting barges were emptied, with the whole scene reflected in the rippling, mirrored surface of the Thames. With the last rays of the sun, those fading images were captured on the river for the smallest fraction of a second. In a moment too brief to be measured, reflections fragmented in the constant movement of the water and sank to the depths to be lost with the billions of other scenes witnessed by the river over a very long life. The Thames is ancient, somewhere between 140 and 170 million years old. It was once a tributary of the Rhine when the land was joined. Through the years, the river has flowed on and on, unconcerned by the human attempts to tame it.

On that golden evening, long ago, at the Lambeth Palace jetty Archbishop Pole's barges could be seen floating quietly, tethered to their moorings. Ceremonial banners would have been carefully folded and stored; the wooden oars neatly stowed away. The haughty voice rings out once more, 'You! Do something with this at once and be quick about it!'

The words are shouted across the dark evening air as the attentive gardener of those times stirs from his evening reverie. Without noticing, he brushes a few stray threads of grass from his smock and then gathers up the branches thrown towards him, checking them over quickly and noting that they are somehow still alive. Who would ever have thought it? Those bits of fig tree had survived the long and difficult journey. But even so, who could expect a few feeble branches stuck in small clay pots to ever be seen again? Surely they would soon be forgotten.

It didn't turn out that way at all. The Vatican fig thrived in its new northern home and is still growing strong at Lambeth Palace today in the main courtyard, more than 450 years later – three very big trees that look to have fused into one. Beyond the palace walls, there were so many threats that might have engulfed London in those four and a half centuries – various waves of the Black Death, a Civil War, the Great Fire. But through it all the fig tree kept growing. There were two world wars as well, and in the second one, parts of the palace were hit by firebombs. The tree escaped and continued on with its own cycles, just as it does today.

Back in 2014, the extraordinary journey of this extraordinary plant took another turn when Archbishop Justin Welby took a rooted cutting with him as a gift when meeting with Pope Francis at the Vatican, so completing the circle by returning a part of the Vatican's tree back to its home. Whether the original fig is still surviving there is uncertain, but perhaps one of my fellow gardeners there might know something about it. Maybe I should write and ask.

More recently, in February 2022, we carried out a ceremonial planting of three more fig trees, which were layered cuttings from the original. This took place to honour Queen Elizabeth II and to serve as a small part of the Green Canopy of trees being planted across the country to celebrate her Platinum Jubilee. For the planting site, I chose the centre of the lawn in the first courtyard so everyone coming through the entrance gate would be greeted by the sight of the fig trees, which have been so closely associated with Lambeth Palace through the centuries. All being well, eventually the old Great Hall should be flanked on either side by figs, and anyone standing in that vast seventeenth-century chamber might see the soft green leaves moving in the breeze through the leaded windows, the trees almost talking to each other like child and parent over the roof of the building.

Perhaps this ceremonial planting could be followed soon by the planting of a fig tree outside Redditch Mosque, as suggested by Sergeant Major Khan. I would very much like to see that. In his letter asking about the tree at Lambeth, he mentioned a passage from the Qur'an that starts with the verse 'By the Fig and the Olive' (Qur'an 95:1), drawing a close connection between these two sacred plants.

Across many different countries and cultures, to 'extend an olive branch' has for centuries been recognised as a unifying gesture of peace and reconciliation, especially after a time of conflict. It was a symbolic act witnessed long ago in ancient Greece and across the Roman Empire, possibly to show that the bearer of the branch was not holding a weapon and had come without any violent thoughts in mind. These days, the olive branch can be seen on coins, national flags and emblems, while to offer an olive branch is still widely accepted as a symbolic show of goodwill, a wish to make amends for wrongs that have been done.

As part of the first lunar landing in 1969, astronaut Neil Armstrong became the first person to walk on the surface of the moon. He had a solid gold replica of an olive branch with him, which he placed on the moon's surface, perhaps with the intention to send a message back to Earth that the exploration of outer space was not part of a wider conflict with the Soviet Union and its allies but being carried out in the interests of science and progress; a peaceful mission with the aim of trying to discover more about the unknown. It is strange to think of that golden olive branch still up there somewhere, hidden under layers of moon dust.

However, I seem to have got a bit distracted here, thinking about space rockets and astronauts and the surface of the moon. Back to Earth and back to Lambeth Palace, where I am now standing on the wide gravel path flanked on each side by a row of olive trees.

It is not a botanical collection of different types. They are all the same species, *Olea europea*. Each tree is intended to represent a province of the Anglican Communion, with a small oak label giving the name of the province, starting with Aotearoa, the Maori name for New Zealand, and continuing in alphabetical order to the West Indies. These olives could be here in the garden for a long time. As the years go by, they will grow so that the trunks thicken to become more and more gnarled and wizened, which should be something quite amazing to see.

As for the oldest living olive tree in the world, many claims have been made for that distinction. There is one near Bethlehem that is said to be more than 4,000 years old but that has not been proved yet. A huge tree in Crete has undergone analysis of its rings, which have confirmed it is at least 2,000 years old, although it could be much older. The usual tests to identify the age of individual trees using radioisotopes were not possible with this one as the heartwood in the middle of the main trunk has decayed over so many years. But it still produces olive fruits every summer.

The ones at Lambeth Palace are all growing in oak barrels at the moment but before too long, maybe in a year or two, they will have to be taken out and planted in the ground, which is where they should be, and where the roots can get a proper chance in the stony earth. I don't think it is a good idea to keep trees in containers for too long, the roots run out of space and the whole plant suffers from the consequences of that. It will be an exciting day when the planting of those olives can be done, and hopefully that day will come soon.

The olive tree can also represent a hope for the future. In the Bible, a dove flew to the Ark '... and the dove came in to him at eventide and, lo, in her mouth an olive leaf plucked off: so Noah knew that the waters were abated from off the earth' (Genesis 8:11). How would it feel to sense the light coming into a dark place after so long, to hear the flutter and beat of a dove's wings against the evening tide, to see the fresh silver green of olive leaves and know that, at last, the worst must be over, things could begin again in a new way?

A WILD ORCHID

Earlier this morning, I found a picture in a book of an Egyptian tomb painting from around 1500 BC. Towards the centre of the image there are two gardeners holding a small rake in each hand. At least, the implements look like rakes, but maybe they are something else, maybe intended for another purpose altogether. Those two painted gardeners are poised with their garden tools, and if they are rakes, I am wondering how they would prepare a path two-handed like that, a path made of sand or gravel. I wonder how it would be done, grading and levelling, all the while listening carefully to the double sound of the rake tines moving across the ground.

The Egyptian tomb painting is filled with trees. Date palms I can see, for certain, and there are avocados, along with what appear to be acacias. There are plenty of clay pots as well, but I can't figure out what could be growing in them. It looks like something geometric and impossible; something made of triangles and circles and nothing like any plant I have seen before.

The left side breaks the symmetry of the composition to show a large rectangular pond. A funeral barge floats there, bringing the deceased through water that is shimmering in blue and green. A solemn figure at the stern indicates the way forward, while a pair of wooden rowing oars are shown at the front of the barge – tantalising, as they are balanced in empty space with nobody working them. Everything seems serene.

There is a wall around that Egyptian garden, faintly visible at the top of the painting. It is an idea found in many gardens in different times and places across the world; the idea of the garden as an enclosed space, to create a safe inner world protected from the wilderness beyond by fences, palisades or some other barrier. Perhaps those early Egyptians with their double rakes needed their wall to guard against some of the surrounding landscape's dangers, to protect their garden from armed marauders or maybe from hostile wild creatures roaming out in the desert. The wall would also help to shield the garden from the damage caused by the harsh, burning winds that would come speeding across the sand dunes. Those gardeners have remained where they are through the centuries, shaded from the heat by the painted trees around them, standing by the cool water of their painted lake and protected by their high walls.

At Lambeth Palace, the garden is also surrounded on most sides by high walls. Some of the earliest versions of these structures were probably built towards the end of the twelfth century, allowing the founding communities of those times to live and worship in a sheltered place where they would be safe from the various threats that might come from outside, with the garden planned as a sanctuary or haven all those centuries ago.

The kinds of threats we are facing around us these days are a bit different from those back then – the quality of the air, for one thing, the pollution and continuous noise from traffic. It is not the worst in London, but hardly what anyone would want either.

Walking through the garden today in early summer, it does not feel as if anything is wrong. The plants are continuing in their own way, the birds are singing as loud and carefree as could be hoped for and there are plenty of insects on the wing. A thunderstorm hurried through here yesterday but this morning there are only broken branches and torn leaf debris as witnesses to that. Everything looks fine.

For the last few years, we have been gardening here with the idea that space should be given to wildlife and habitat provided, whether that is a hedge, a decaying log or something else. Growing plenty of plants of different types offers more opportunities for wildlife, with plantings everywhere – as many as possible. The garden is a place to be shared and it is not only for humans but wild creatures as well.

It is good to see how much is going on this morning. Whatever happens, nature does seem to find a way to manage and keep moving, changing and improvising when needed, while never quite repeating. Through adaptation, many kinds of plants and wild creatures have found a place in this unpromising urban terrain; a place where they can thrive within these high garden walls, right here, in the middle of one of the world's biggest and busiest cities.

As I walk slowly along the gravel path, from around a corner a small black figure appears. It is a cat, maybe not so wild as some of the other inhabitants of the garden but still a creature of significance. She turned up here as a stray a couple of years ago. I think she probably wandered away from her home and got lost, or maybe was left abandoned in the park next door and did her best to fend for herself for a while, managing for a few weeks at least. Somehow, she must have realised there was a better place for her beyond the high partition, that there was this other green world through there, a big garden alongside the park. She made her way in via a small gap in the fencing. Back then, she was very timid and thin with some fur on her head but not much on her body. Her big sage-coloured eyes were full of fear and for those first few days it was difficult to get anywhere near as she would just run away at top speed. Then, with a more regular supply of food and somewhere warm to sleep, she began to recover, and with her self-confidence returning, she began to exert her own influence over the garden.

Yesterday afternoon the sun was shining and it was warm, but she must have sensed a change was coming and took herself away to one of the various secret shelters she has located around the place. And, sure enough, she was right. The weather turned without any warning and from nowhere the sky darkened to a deep, bruised metal, while a strange violet light coloured the air.

After a sudden shudder, tremendous crashes of thunder sounded, followed quickly by cracks of sheet lightning. The angry thunder rolled again with more lightning. A storm had come from nowhere and it was magnificent.

Or at least, it would have been magnificent if I hadn't been caught up right in the middle of it. The flashing spears of bolt lightning can be deadly, but sheet lightning is caused by bolts breaking out inside the clouds and so should not be harmful to anything below. I couldn't remember what to do, I couldn't concentrate with all the noise and white light.

Then the rain began, coming down hard. I tried to keep out of it by standing under one of the big yew trees near the compost heap but that was no good. I shouldn't be under a tree in this kind of storm, lightning will always take the quickest route to the ground. No, I should be kneeling in a low dip with higher ground above me – that's how it should be done, to wait there in the low area for the danger to pass.

But with the rain hammering down and all the commotion around, it was difficult to think properly. So instead, I just made a run for it. I went splashing along the gravel path, my clothes drenched in no time and sticking to my skin. I staggered past the herb garden, turned the corner to the wider path flanked by the lines of olive trees. They were all just damp shapes blurring to each side as I hurried on. The air was turning to liquid and there were different colours from violet to purple, with odd patterns appearing as the storm pressed down closer.

Dark stains were streaking down the yellow sandstone of the palace building. Chunks of masonry have been falling from those walls these last few years, some of them quite big. Water gets absorbed by the soft sandstone and when it freezes the water expands, which leads to fractures, causing bits of the building to break away. Maybe, one day soon, the whole thing will crumble to the ground. But probably not today.

There was no time to think about any of that, I just had to keep moving. I had to get out of the rain as quickly as I could. Another flash of lightning came with more thunder rapidly following. The storm was still directly above and not moving away. I had made a mistake to be caught out in the open, to be caught out there on the path. But it was too late, I had to keep going.

There came a sudden wind squall and hundreds of leaves that were not ready to fall were torn from branches and strewn everywhere. A giant plane tree bowed down to touch the ground and then stood tall again. Somewhere nearby, a sycamore branch cracked and snapped and slid slowly into the canopy, the weight of the heavy broken branch resting suspended there.

The rain had soaked through my boots, my socks squelching as I ran and ran, moving as if in slow motion but getting nearer to some cover as I made for the potting shed beside the greenhouse. From the corner of my eye, I saw a small smudge of soft pink down in the wet grass by the quince tree and, out of breath, I stopped to take a closer look. That little pink smudge turned out to be a wild orchid – a pyramidal orchid – alone in the rain but happy enough, having found some shelter in the long grass beneath the old quince tree. It felt like a little miracle, a moment that makes everything worthwhile, as if the storm clouds had lifted slightly to cause the rain to retreat for a moment.

From a dry vantage point under the nearby lean-to where the bikes are stored, the cat was watching me. She saw me on my knees where the ground falls away. She watched me examining that pink pyramidal orchid in the grass as the rain came back stronger and poured down in torrents all around me.

I turned away to face the shed, which was still a little way off. Water was chugging down the drainpipes, which were streaming and unable to cope with the flood. I saw two rakes left outside by accident, rain streaming down their handles as they leant up against the wooden shed. Quickly, I got up, walked the short distance and went to shelter inside. As I stood there, still breathing hard, dripping and soaked through, I listened to the steady thrum of rain on the roof above me.

I was wondering what to do next when I noticed a tiny mouse sauntering out from behind a stack of clay pots in the corner. He or she looked up at me casually, then looked at the deluge outside the open door before scuttling back to the safety of the dry shadows with their comforting musty smells of old compost.

So, there we were, the four of us, a few metres apart, all seeking shelter in our different ways. The mouse in the hidden corner, the cat under the lean-to, the wild orchid beneath the quince tree and me, protected by the wooden surrounds of the shed. We would all have to wait it out. For me, in my shed, there wasn't anything to do, nothing to read, except for a long list of seeds that was pinned to the wall, seeds that should be sown one day soon. The shed has a little window and that could have been cleaner, it was true. The glass pane was streaked with water drops, bright raindrops full of life. The time went by and eventually the rain came to an end.

EARLY DAYS

When I am giving a guided tour, at some point near the beginning I usually mention that the garden was first founded in 1197, the same year as Lambeth Palace itself, according to the official records. This information is usually met without question and occasionally I have even heard a quiet gasp from the small group around me; maybe some of them are taken aback at the thought of all those centuries of gardening. In my role as a guide, I realise I might have gone a little too far at times by suggesting that before 1197 there was nothing much to find on the site, implying it was no more than a barren marsh beside an unpromising stretch of the River Thames. Not much was going on, I would intimate, it was just a bleak place of little interest, flat and prone to flooding.

At some point in the 1190s, for various reasons, some of which seem to have been political, the idea came to create something significant here on the sticky marsh alongside the existing wooden church that eventually became St Mary's at Lambeth. The proposal was to build a new palace with a chapel and high stone towers, a wonder beyond imagination rising up from the swamp.

It is hard to say for certain what those first structures might have looked like because few recorded details seem to have survived beyond the deeds describing the purchase of lands for the Archbishop of Canterbury. While so much is unknown, at least there are a few things we can glean concerning the garden from one of the oldest court roles for Lambeth dated 1237, a copy of which can be found in the Lambeth Palace Library archives.

The court role records that the palace already had significant orchards, with surplus pears and other fruits being sold to local residents at the main gate. A new herbarium had just been constructed and, in another part of the grounds, hemp and flax were being sown as crops. I saw a beautiful blue flax flower just yesterday, growing wild in the garden. I suppose it could not be some distant relative of those thirteenth-century flax, although I would like to think that it was.

Moving on from that 1237 court role, another record dated 1322 can be found in the archives, telling of a new wall being constructed around the grounds and the establishment of a rabbit field towards the north end. The rabbits must have been introduced as a food supply, even though meat was not generally approved of in medieval monastic life. A fish or a hen's egg was allowed, now and then, but meat was only to be taken on rare occasions.

It is also recorded in the 1322 note that a labouring boy was hired for eight days to dig out 'flowering plants'. I wonder why they were digging out flowering plants back then. It could be they meant something that would be described these days as weeds, a term derived from Anglo-Saxon and in use back then, although, to many, it would often have meant either grass or a herb. A plant growing in the wrong place is often defined as a weed, posing a question any gardener anywhere in the world has to consider – which plants are allowed into the garden and which are not?

Maybe the hired garden boy mentioned in the note of 700 years ago was pulling out things like leopard's bane, sow thistle or cat's ear, just as some of the garden team were doing here in the same space only last week. Those weeds mentioned are tenacious plants that endure through many years and that is why they are such good survivors. You can never quite get rid of them, not even if you really want to.

But where did he come from, that gardening boy of 1322? Where did he live? The area around the medieval Lambeth Palace was fairly sparsely populated, most of the local dwellings being humble structures somewhere along the riverbank, although there were some well-established towns or villages nearby. There was Camberwell and Chenintune, which became known as Kennington, also Brixieton, now Brixton.

As dawn was breaking, he must have trudged along the cold, muddy tracks to work at this strange place with stone towers and vast gardens, all built on the dank marshlands. Trying to fit in with the peculiar ways of the garden team, set to work pulling up plants or digging them out from the herb garden or the many raised beds where vegetables were growing, he must have had to learn very quickly which of those plants were wanted and which were not. When he looked up, all around the garden area he would have seen the newly built high wall made of stone, topped with a neat finish of fresh thatching. But there would be no time to linger for the boy to admire his surroundings, he had to get back to work and, with luck, those few days of labour might lead to full-time employment for him if things went well.

From the archived record we know that he was paid a penny for each of the eight days he was said to have been there. It might not sound much, but those were hard years to live through. From 1314 to 1316, wild storms and almost perpetual rain had devastated food supplies in England and much of Europe, the terrible weather causing what became known as the Great Famine. Prices were very high and essentials such as bread were difficult to find. They were years of suffering and there are many stories of parents abandoning their children when they could no longer care for them.

Perhaps the gardening boy was a child in that situation trying to fend for himself alone? Whatever the case, the eight pennies he earned for his labour would probably have been of great help, at least for a while. In the London of those years, a skilled worker could earn around sixpence a day. Sixpence was just enough to buy a pair of basic shoes made from thin leather.

When the boy made his brief 1322 appearance in the story of Lambeth Palace, the garden around him was already several hundred years old. The founding date of 1197 often quoted in books and by me in my guided tours is not accurate, for there is another history which tells that the first Lambeth Palace was built on the site of a Saxon manor that had been the property of Edward the Confessor's sister, Goda. The Domesday Book lists Lambeth, or Lanchei, as belonging to her in 1066. On Christmas Day of that year, William the Conqueror was crowned King of England in Westminster Abbey and, among other properties, Goda's manor and its grounds were seized by him and given to a community of Benedictine monks from Rochester, who laid out a large garden where they grew produce for their kitchen, as well as herbs and flowers.

Those monks must have cultivated and looked after the ground here for more than a century before the manor was eventually acquired for Archbishop Baldwin in 1190 as a site to construct the large dwelling that became Lambeth Palace. The existing garden created by the Benedictine monks would have contained orchards with various fruit trees, all carefully pruned, and there would have been extensive raised plots for growing the many vegetables and herbs that were needed. Cut lawns also had to be provided for relaxing walks and, most likely, a fountain would have been located somewhere close to the chapel, both for washing and as a place for contemplation while listening to the play of the bubbling water and looking down into the stillness of the small pond below. Other secluded smaller spaces had to be created within the main garden, places for quiet retreat to pray or to meditate, but also spaces for the Benedictine monks to withdraw from the group if they needed to, giving them a safe place to aid recovery from illness and infirmity, both mental and physical.

Saint Benedict wrote that 'the lovely green of herb or tree' would provide comfort and nourishment for those in difficulty. In AD 516, he completed a book of seventy-three short chapters, which became known as *The Rule of Saint Benedict*, an influential document that provided a framework for the organisation and running of a monastery. The advice given there continues to be of relevance to sacred sites in many parts of the world, even fifteen centuries later.

Archbishop Justin told me that he takes time to study *The Rule of Saint Benedict* most days. Several years ago, he founded the Community of Saint Anselm at Lambeth Palace, the idea being to allow a group of up to twenty young people from all different parts of the world to live together in residence for a term of twelve months. Anselm was a follower of Saint Benedict and the newly established community at Lambeth has the *Rule of Saint Benedict* as a guide.

From time to time, some of the members of the community help out in the garden. Finding volunteer work beyond the walls has been difficult this spring, so they have been doing a lot more gardening in the grounds than might have been expected, weeding and tidying the gravel paths, clearing tree debris after high winds and so on.

They also helped to save some of the hundreds of seedlings we had been growing in the greenhouse. Alice had sown these seeds in February and most of them had begun to germinate as hoped towards the end of March. There was the danger that without some attention those new seedlings would just fry under the glass and get no further than putting out their first pairs of delicate leaves. The time we had to tend to them was unexpectedly limited, and it was difficult to keep up and do what had to be done.

The Community of St Anselm members had been asking if there were any other chores they could help with, just to keep things going somehow, so early one April morning, I gave them a short tutorial on how to transplant seedlings and then left them to get on with it, hoping for the best. Over the next few days, they gently moved the fragile new plants from the trays into pots, where they would at least have more of a chance to survive and maybe grow into something we could plant outside as the weather began to warm up.

Over the winter months, Alice had searched through the catalogues and carefully selected the range of seeds that were to be sown, mostly vegetables. We had grown some in the past but it had all become fairly haphazard and sporadic, so she made a more organised plan to include proper traditional crop rotation. With all that in mind, as the days got longer in February, we dug out some new small vegetable beds in preparation and composted them well. The seeds sown in the greenhouse included plenty of legumes, beans and peas, as well as courgettes, sweetcorn, carrots, beetroot, celeriac and sweet pumpkin.

Another idea was to grow some colourful annual climbers and allow them to scramble up some old metal supports we had found, which were not being used. These would be placed in the Chapel Garden among the herbs to provide some vertical lines to contrast with the dominant horizontals of the grey and green aromatic plantings. I hoped they would be small explosions of colour, like living fireworks. There were seeds of morning glories, sprawling orange nasturtiums, purple cup and saucer plants, as well as a few other surprises. With the help from the Community of Saint Anselm, maybe not all but at least some of those climber seedlings were saved and given the chance to grow and show off their vibrant flower colours later in the year.

When I was a younger gardener, I could hardly wait for the process of germination to begin. Every morning I would go into the greenhouse and inspect the newly sown trays, getting down on my knees to look across them on a level to see if I could spy the first signs of green breaking the dark surface. There is something about the atmosphere inside a greenhouse, something about the air, and my senses seem somehow more alive. Maybe it is the light coming through the glass, the smells of compost, sand and gravel, and then, in spring especially, the feeling of new energy hurrying into life all around the enclosed space. I have spent some of the happiest hours of my life in greenhouses.

Standing for a few moments in the one at Lambeth Palace, I am taken back in time to some of the other greenhouses I have known. They all seem to be connected by an invisible thread. Where I grew up, we had a very small one by the back door and one of my first memories as a child is looking up at some grapes growing way above my head. It was warm in there, gazing up at the strange bunches of grapes, pale pink with a faint grey bloom on the surface, as if they were made of frosted glass and might be cold to touch. But I couldn't tell, they were too high above me. I couldn't reach that high to touch their glassy surfaces.

Later, I was to work in several fine greenhouses and grew all kinds of things there. The present one at Lambeth Palace is probably the most basic I have ever seen in a historic garden, although there must have been quite a few other, grander structures sited here that came and went over the centuries.

When the celebrated gardener and diarist John Evelyn visited the palace on 28 December 1691, he saw a new greenhouse that had recently been constructed. He described it as an impressive thing, made in three sections, with a stove in the middle, also mentioning that oranges and lemons had already been grown under the glass with some success. Being the last week of the year, perhaps the winter day of his visit was bitter and cold, so the warmth in the new greenhouse would be welcome, for he particularly made mention that the stove was working very well.

John Evelyn wrote various books, several with horticulture as the main subject. In 1664, he published *Sylva*, which is about the widespread felling of woodlands to serve industry and commerce. He called on King William III in the preface to oblige landowners to plant millions more trees and to halt the deforestation. The book includes engravings of appropriate trees to plant and illustrations of their foliage to help with identification.

There is no record telling what he made of the garden on that December day in 1691, but I wonder if he spoke to any of the gardeners. That might have been a fascinating conversation. The seventeenth-century greenhouse was said to have had all the style and advantages of its time, but its location is unknown and no account of what happened to it has survived. Looking again at the little greenhouse we have today, I couldn't say it has all that much style nor too many advantages. Perhaps it may not be the best, but it works well enough for us, and sometimes it is just a question of getting by and making do.

THE TULIP TREE

There are two tulip trees growing in the garden, both nearly as tall as the tallest of the surrounding buildings. No record exists of either being planted but they look to be of a similar age, maybe 100 years old or so. They are fast-growing trees, which means it can be difficult to say for certain what age they might be.

The other day in the garden office, I was sorting through some box files that are kept on the shelves. I was looking for a particular document, although I don't remember now what it was I wanted. In my search, I came across a small colour photograph showing the tulip tree on the main lawn, taken in the late 1970s or around then, I would guess, from the look of the print with its colours slightly washed out and the focus slightly blurred. The tree appears quite small in the photo, dwarfed by the familiar building behind. So, I think my estimate that it was at least a century old was probably an exaggeration.

In the early summer, tulip trees are usually to be seen festooned with hundreds of small cup-shaped flowers, pale yellow blooms flared with orange at the base. In a vague way, they do look a little like small tulips, reminding me of another kind of tree, the cup shape of the flowers resembling those of a magnolia. The two are related, both coming from the same plant family, Magnoliaceae. Magnolias are usually thought of as being trees indigenous to Asia, especially the Himalayas. That is true, but they have another zone they are native to – the eastern areas of North America, which is also home to the tulip tree. It can be found up and down the east coast, often growing wild all the way from Florida in the south to the much colder climate of Ontario, over the Canadian border.

In April 1607, a small group of ships from England sailed towards that east coast of the immense land mass that was to become North America. They were some of the first ships to complete the demanding voyage across the Atlantic and were making for the area now known as Virginia.

With the journey seeming to be at an end and the heavy anchor dropped at last, maybe some of those passengers and crew crowded together on the deck to get a first look at the shoreline that had appeared before them. After so much relentless grey and blue through the months of the ocean crossing, the green on the horizon must have been a welcome sight. Worn out and shattered by the long voyage into the unknown, perhaps some of them gazed through the still air and noticed a few unusual trees standing tall over on the land. Maybe they even glimpsed the yellow and orange colours visible through the green leaves. It was coming to the end of spring after all, nearly flowering time for the tulip tree, and some early blooms might have been showing.

More likely, those passengers and crew would have been way too tired to make much sense of the new surroundings, their nerves all jangling from the long journey. There would have been so many things to take in, so many peculiar things after six or seven hard weeks rocking on the ocean, cramped tight inside narrow wooden vessels. How strange it must have been for the indigenous people on the land back then to watch from the thickets of pine, hickory and oak as the giant ships moved slowly closer, cleaving through the water with their vast sails fluttering quietly in the gentle breeze. Did those people look on in wonder? Did they have any sense of the devastating changes that would be brought by those weird newcomers aboard those weird wooden craft?

A settlement was founded and named Jamestown, after the English king of the time. The first few years were tough, partly because those first incomers had chosen a site where it was difficult to grow much, and to make things worse, they were continually plagued by swarms of mosquitos from the nearby swamps. Of the 104 colonists who arrived in 1607, only thirty-eight survived the first winter. In the next few decades, more and more men and women arrived to try to make a new life in the new colony. In those early years, disease and hunger were never far away and there were even tales of cannibalism.

Further problems came as the new arrivals confronted the native people in various bloody and costly skirmishes, which achieved little other than to breed hostility and suspicion on both sides. Even so, somehow, the settlers managed to hang on and their numbers began to steadily increase as, each year, more ships arrived from the Old World.

A little over thirty years after that first landing, a boat arrived from England carrying John Tradescant the Younger, a gardener and collector who is still famed in gardening today. The date of his voyage is not certain but it seems most likely to have been in the autumn of 1637.

The journey would have been arduous, tucked into a berth much too small for him, the usual fare for the berth at the time being £5 – a lot of money. Conditions were made worse because passengers were often obliged to spend most of the time below decks, crowded together in the darkness of the hold. They got by on a diet of dry biscuits, peas and oatmeal, although it was recommended that each traveller bring a gallon of brandy as well. They lay on coarse canvas sheets under thick blankets, which were repeatedly soaked by the salt water that was never far away. Washing must have been tricky in those fetid conditions, just keeping body and soul together must have been difficult. Beyond the thin, wooden casing of the ship, the creak of cables and ropes could be heard, along with the ceaseless slapping and churning of the waves.

The weeks on the ocean went by and, like so many others, John Tradescant the Younger survived the hardships and arrived safely at the harbour, where the first thing would be to seek lodgings and a place to rest. How the land must have swayed beneath his feet as he took his first steps ashore, the rocking motion of the waves still with him.

He appears to have stayed through to the summer of the following year, 1638, but information regarding his visit to Jamestown is hard to come by. Very little was recorded of what went on in those times. If he kept a diary or a journal to note down his impressions, nothing of that has come to light so far and none of the letters he may have written home have survived. So, we will never know what he made of the crumbling wooden warehouse that was the first sight for most arrivals to Jamestown in that year. We will never know if he involved himself in the rumoured drunkenness and gambling described by others as rife in the east coast settlements of that time.

Standing jostled by the crowd on the deck, England must have seemed a long way behind him – a world away. His wife Jane had died three years earlier. Their two children were still very young and he must have known it was quite possible he would never see them again.

But perhaps the day he landed in Virginia was a bright one as the ship came gliding in over the still water towards the raggedy dock. Hundreds of green trees were on the land just ahead, beginning to turn to their autumn colours of brown, orange and gold. His clothes would be caked stiff with sweat and brine, and maybe he shivered as the ship swayed in a sudden gust, wondered at its power, the way it kept pushing on unfaltering even after such a long voyage, pressing so many thousands of fathoms of water down beneath its keel. The anchor chain descending loudly would send another shudder through everything, while the agitated hubbub of nervous voices grew in volume around him, jubilation at having got there in one piece mixed with fear of the unknown that lay ahead.

The aim of his expedition was to gather up all kinds of rarities – whatever could be found – flowers, seeds, plants and shells, as well as artefacts from the indigenous people. Beads and weapons, rugs and shawls – anything strange would be good. These were the curiosities he wanted to take back with him to London to augment the family collection of extraordinary things that they were keeping and displaying in Lambeth. They needed to encourage paying visitors to come to the place in Vauxhall they called 'the Ark', the Musaeum Tradescantium, opened in 1634 and housed inside a building rented from the Dean and Chapter of Canterbury and sited less than a mile from Lambeth Palace.

The collection included marvels from nature as well as crafted objects. If you paid your entrance fee, you might have seen various kinds of fossils, a display of unusual shoes, pressed plants and dried insects, some jewels as well as 'phoenix feathers' and 'dragons' eggs'. You might even have been shown a set of gambling dice the colour of ice, shot through with traces of blue.

In the Tradescant displays, amazing shields and costumes could be admired or possibly a handmade flute, carved from an unknown type of wood and able to play notes by itself, melodies haunting and melancholic like nothing ever heard before – all kinds of spectacular things, for all possible uses. But over and above everything, it should be remembered that both father and son were highly skilled gardeners with the most prized items of their collection being the living plants that could be found growing in the garden beside their Lambeth house.

From the trip to Virginia, the younger Tradescant brought back more than 200 different specimens to introduce to that garden, from swamp cypress and red columbine to red maple. Many of them were collected from the marshy thickets by the woodland streams, but it is not known if he collected these seeds and specimens himself or if others provided them on request. Whatever the case, among the most significant of the living treasures he brought back from Virginia were the cuttings of the tulip tree and its seeds.

The settlers in the New World had a different name for it, they called it 'canoewood', having noticed how the indigenous people favoured the timber to make their skiffs and boats because they knew from experience that it was especially buoyant. Perhaps John Tradescant himself travelled the adjacent rivers and swamps around Jamestown in one of those tulip tree boats as he looked for rare and unusual plants to collect. The pale wood of the hull would have moved through the dark water with the sound of the paddles gently plashing at the brown surface, pushing through the eddying currents. When the guide indicated a place to stop and search for particular plants, he had to wince as he stepped from the skiff onto the shore, feeling his feet squelch in the soggy ground as the muddy swamp water seeped into his good-for-nothing boots. The path pointed out by his guide was usually invisible to the eye and blocked by a mass of fallen tree trunks, the sharp ends of broken branches making jags and snags, painful as they caught and pierced his skin.

Back in the canoe, with samples and cuttings stuffed into all available pockets, there would be so many strange things to see and hear. He was bitten again and again by insects, while invisible creatures watched on from the covering stands of heavy vegetation to each side. In that strange place everything was very different to the way it might have seemed. Strange noises were coming from the shadows, a sudden echoing howl and then quiet. Overhead, birds that were difficult to identify would arch and glide across the empty sky where smoke trails were drifting, the last light stirring as dusk began to come down.

Soon the sky would be alive with scatterings of stars. Everything might well have been different in that strange land but they were the same constellations that shone over Lambeth; the same stars that sparkled in the night sky over far away London. Maybe he could have stayed at home after all, in the safety of his garden, and just imagined what this 'new world' that he had heard so much talk about might be like, so many rumours, both true and false.

The long return voyage back to England in 1638 may not have been as hard going as the outward journey, with following winds to help push the ship along more quickly. On reaching London, he found that his father had died a few months before, while he had been on the other side of the ocean. Somehow, the older man's celebrated gardening reputation had always seemed to overshadow the achievements of his only son, and now there would be no chance for the younger man to show his father the various treasures and wonderful finds he had brought back with him from his intrepid adventures on the other side of the ocean.

These days, something of the Tradescant family still remains in the Vauxhall area. Their family home that housed the collections of their Ark was demolished long ago and other buildings stand there now at the junction of Tradescant Road and Walberswick Street. There is no longer any trace of their garden. Both John the Younger and John the Elder are buried just outside the grounds of Lambeth Palace in the cemetery of the Church of St Mary, where their intricately carved tomb can still be visited in the churchyard, now part of the Garden Museum. As for the many different plants they brought to England from their journeys far afield and the ones they obtained through trading or purchase, thousands of those can still be found growing in parks and gardens all across the country.

I have looked after a few tulip trees in all the places I have worked and they are beautiful things, but each one has been damaged or broken by high winds and rain storms in one way or another. Although they are a hardwood, they can be quite brittle because they grow so quickly. That said, looking at the tree on the main lawn at Lambeth Palace, I can see it is well balanced and intact, almost a pyramid and a perfect example of its type. It is wonderful in flower right now, in early summer, with the promise of autumn colours later on, all golden and copper brown. When winter comes and all the leaves have fallen, the weathered wood of the trunk becomes more visible, the bark showing a slight but definite twist, patterned here and there with felty moss and lichen.

I place my hand for a moment on that bark where the tree trunk twists and I can hear a humming sound all around me. It is early June and hundreds of bees have crawled into the cupped tulip flowers of the tree to gather the nectar and they buzz away as they work with the sound made louder by the shape of the flower, each bee inside its own amplifier.

Sometimes, when there are visitors around, this is a good place to set up some tables and chairs to take in the afternoon in the cool shade as the light filters down through the leaves. This summer, I have moved one of the garden benches and placed it here under the tulip tree. Moving a bench to a different position can open up new views, it can provide another way of looking and give an unexpected angle on those same old things we might think we know only too well.

When visiting gardens, I think maybe we stride around a bit too much, trying to take it all in as eager consumers and making sure we don't miss a single thing. As the years have gone by, I tend not to look at garden maps when visiting a place that is new to me, although I might buy one and check the various routes and areas when I am back at home later on. It could be I do this so as not to feel everything has to be revealed all at once, that there are garden paths I might not walk along at all, and those paths not taken might be of just as much interest as the paths I did explore.

When travelling in Persia in the 1660s, the jeweller Sir John Chardin noted:

> The Persians don't walk so much in gardens as we do but content themselves with a bare prospect and breathing the fresh air ... for this end they set themselves down in some part of the garden, at their first coming into it, and never move their seats till they are coming out of it.

Perhaps the precious hour spent on a bench or sitting quietly somewhere else allows the garden to come to you in its own way. You might find there are all kinds of unexpected things going on if you give them time and space.

Sitting on the steps leading up to the Terrace and studying the tulip tree again from more of a distance, I am still surprised at how undamaged and untouched it has been by all the many winters of rough weather. Maybe the other trees have sheltered this one from the worst of it, or perhaps it is the height of the buildings that have provided protection. A few of the branches break now and then but nothing too serious. Sometimes, I have to get the tall ladder out to climb up and free the broken branches from the canopy.

IN THE LABYRINTH

The Company of Gardeners was first referred to in the London City Corporation records in 1345. It was founded as a guild with the main objective being to provide a preparation for young people to enter the profession of gardening via a seven-year apprenticeship. Through that long period of training the apprentices would learn a wide range of techniques and practices, with the intriguing promise on completion of being immersed and fully skilled in 'the crafte, trade and misterie of gardening'.

While mowing the turf labyrinth at the far end of the garden earlier today, I was wondering about those seven years of training, about the parts that talked of the craft and the mystery. For this kind of specialised grass cutting that I have been doing here this afternoon for the labyrinth, I think something would have been included in the Company of Gardeners' extensive syllabus.

Grass labyrinths or turf mazes were around in gardens back then, and there is a definite craft needed to care for them; an assurance and skill that is required when using a sickle or a scythe – or a mower, in more modern times. But there is still the mystery the Company speaks of. Could all the hidden secrets of gardening be discovered, even after seven long years as an apprentice? Would the true mysteries be revealed? But maybe it was a different kind of mystery they were thinking of.

Returning to look at the labyrinth at Lambeth Palace, I am thinking how visitors on guided tours sometimes say to me that it must be quite hard to look after a lawn feature like that, a tricky maze of paths with no straight lines, just circles inside circles. How exacting it must be to cut that spiral shape with precision and manage it all without making a mistake. A little misjudgement, a little mis-step or loss of concentration could ruin the whole thing in an instant. After listening to them speak, I usually take a deep breath and sigh quietly before looking off into the distance to consider the complexity of such a question, to carefully weigh up the difficulty of such a mowing task.

Then I would have to admit that there is not as much involved as they might think. It is really quite easy. I set the mower deck to a height of level three for the winding pathway, then to level seven for the raised ridges defining that path.

Anyone with a lawn could make a turf labyrinth if they wanted to. If there were no grass, the labyrinth could be made from pebbles or stones laid out in a backyard or something of that kind. Traditionally, turf labyrinths are made by cutting a continuous path, forming a series of connected circles to encourage the walker to walk towards the centre.

A sense of balance and symmetry is needed, but in the end, a labyrinth merely forms a pathway that leads somewhere or nowhere, and where it goes depends on us, to some extent. It can offer a space for reflection and contemplation as we make our way around the spiral. The pressures of time can melt away as we move in silence through the circles, with a new perspective forming at every step along the way as the path continually curves.

There are other types of labyrinths, of course, mazes with narrow paths closed in by high walls or solid green hedges. These can be approached as puzzles or games, trying to fool us with dead ends while throwing in the further confusion of devious twists and turns, sometimes cheating the eye with their bewildering patterns of alleys. They can also be something more sinister than a game. Instead, they can be a trap or a prison, as in the tale of the Minotaur caught in the awful gloom of an elaborate and intricate maze. In that story, the labyrinth is a dark place of pain and torture, a place of brutal sacrifice and punishment.

Back here in the garden and far away from those thoughts, it is a warm summer day and the sun is shining brightly while a few pale pink clouds line up in the sky. The mowing is done for now and the machine can be switched off to allow its engine to rest and tick over quietly. For thousands of years, geometric labyrinth designs in a similar style to the one I was working on have appeared in many different places across the world. Ancient cave paintings have been found, as well as carvings etched into rock faces.

Some of the oldest labyrinths that have survived are just simple stone structures laid out on the ground. So many different cultures, so many separate groups of people who could not have had any contact with each other, still somehow came up with similar designs and ideas: circles inside circles, with a pathway leading from the outside into the centre. How all that could have happened in such comparable ways is quite puzzling. A common theme for these devices seems to have been the idea of meditation and contemplation; the labyrinth providing a place to withdraw, a place to try to free the mind from the material concerns of the everyday world.

A few years ago, in the East Godavari district of India, freelance archaeologist Kadiyala Venkateswara Rao discovered a large painting depicting a labyrinth on a flat stone at the entrance to a hilltop cave. It dates to Neolithic times, which came to an end around 4500 BC. The painting is in good condition despite its great age, comprising seven linked circles in red ochre rendered on a white background. The route through the labyrinth is wide enough to trace with your hand on the surface of the rock. Mr Rao was 75 at the time of the find and could not have been wandering about on that desolate hilltop just by chance; he would surely have heard rumours of the labyrinth painting. What a day it must have been for him when at last he located the cave entrance he had been looking for.

There is some speculation as to its purpose. The cave faces the rising sun, so the hilltop may have been a place of worship for Neolithic hunter-gatherers, which is suggested also by the faint outlines of a bull and a deer to each side of the labyrinth design. A bull and a deer, but no tiger, although they are known to inhabit the East Godavari district. Perhaps they were too fierce and threatening to be painted.

There is the story told by the Buddha, of the tiger's cave where many human footprints may be seen going into the entrance but none coming out. Maybe the tale is intended as a short parable, warning us against the dangers of being overcurious or overconfident in the face of the unknown. Or it could be interpreted as a meditation on nature. Humans have often viewed nature as a kind of resource for their benefit, supposing that the natural world exists for the purpose of being exploited for gain or amusement. The story of the tiger's cave suggests that nature is always wild in essence, never a plaything to be shaped and framed. Nature is the tiger that will devour us in an instant if sufficient respect is not given.

Clearly, Mr Rao did not meet any tigers coming from the cave entrance that he found up in the hills. I have read that the labyrinth design he discovered was perhaps painted to indicate that treasure of great value was stored in the cave, maybe gold and other precious things. But wouldn't it be odd to advertise that to anyone who just happened to be passing by? It's possible the labyrinth painting was just something beautiful to look at and making it had been a good way to pass the time.

Similar geometric designs can be found laid out on the floors of churches throughout Europe, one of the most well known being the labyrinth that was created inside Chartres Cathedral in 1220. Weary pilgrims would enter the church to complete the last part of their long journey, walking the symbolic path built into the cathedral floor, praying as they went and hoping to cast aside any last troubles and cares to finally reach a point of stillness at the cathedral's centre.

The grass labyrinth I have been cutting today is also for contemplation. The idea is to move alone around the seven spirals of the circuit, meditating and reflecting. By the end of the walk, something helpful may have been found – an answer to a troubling question or maybe just a little peace of mind. If it has made no difference, you can always go back and start again. Or try another day.

With the mowing finished, I step back to check that everything is all right. It may not be perfect, but I think the work is good enough, and if the Company of Gardeners should ever come to inspect what I've been doing or should be observing me from somewhere or other, hopefully they would approve and give me a pass mark. As I turn to walk away, the labyrinth does not watch me go. Instead, the single spiral eye gazes up at the summer sky without blinking.

Pushing the mower back towards the garden shed along the gravel path, I walk through a series of soft reds and blues, through the haze of colour that the flower beds have become in June, with all the warmth and recent rainfall at night. There is laughter somewhere nearby, a rustling sound, slightly echoing back on itself in the afternoon air.

A group of the hospital staff from next door are gathered around one of the benches near the wall, smiling at something someone has said. They are holding packets of crisps and big bottles of lemonade, offering some to me as I pass by. It is a hot day, and a cool drink would be nice – the simple act of sharing a cup of lemonade with strangers. I wouldn't have minded a handful of the crisps as well, bright orange and cheese flavoured, quite appealing. But recently I have found anything with cheese or even artificial cheese flavourings bring on the most vivid and unnerving dreams at night, all in supersaturated colours. Those dreams can be quite exhausting.

It is good to see the staff from the hospital relaxing there on the benches in the sunshine, laughing together and sheltered by the greenery of the leaves and trees, surrounded by bright flowers. I wave to them and pass by, but no crisps or lemonade for me today. Moving further on down the path, I see that Alice is there working on a new planting that she organised, one of the ones we planted up at the end of last year. She returned to work recently, walking all the way from Deptford where she lives, 5 miles from door to door. Her new bike should arrive soon and that will make things easier.

These days, there are usually three gardeners looking after the garden, Cheyenne, Alice and me. Before, there probably would have been quite a few more of us. Across the ten centuries this big garden has been here, it could be that some of the many gardeners employed to tend it would have received their training via the Company of Gardeners' seven-year apprenticeship. That seems quite likely to me.

For most of its history, for the first eight of nine centuries or so, the garden was more than twice the present size of 10 acres. In 1901, half of the growing area was given to the London County Council for use by the public.

For ten or twenty years before that, the east part of the site had been regularly used for recreation by the palace's neighbours, for impromptu games of football and so on, most likely without permission. That area had become known to the locals as Lambeth Palace Fields. Maybe to sort out the situation once and for all, there was a final meeting in one of the larger rooms of the palace, perhaps in the Blue Drawing Room overlooking the herb garden. Some at the meeting might have lamented the loss of so much precious ground as they peered out of the blurred windows across the clipped lawns. Others might have argued that this would be for the greater good; giving up half of the garden would provide many people of the surrounding parish with an open outdoor area to greatly improve the quality of their daily lives.

When all the talking was done, eventually a map must have appeared and been spread out on the large wooden table. A ruler and a pencil would have been used to draw a straight line across that map, dividing the garden into two halves, more or less. A map, a ruler, a pencil – a single straight line and it was done. Never mind if a few trees were in the way; we've got to keep that line straight. I don't know what map of the garden they might have used; there are dozens in the archives. I have seen quite a few, some of them fascinating and others inaccurate or improbable, possibly drawn up by cartographers in a hurry.

Meanwhile, after all these garden diversions I find I am still walking along, pushing the mower towards the shed, leaving everything behind. The June heatwave continues but it should break on Friday with the promise of thunderstorms. Sleep does not come easily in this weather, and last night I lay awake through the early hours in the darkened bedroom, my mind whirling but my body too tired to get out of bed. In the shadows, I was looking up at a faint crack in the ceiling above me, and then saw the ceiling slowly rise as the roof began to lift itself from the building. Silently, it lifted up and moved away, evaporating into nothing. I began to float up from the bed towards the dark sky, where I started to drift through the night.

The streets were laid out far below and the local park was deep in shadows. Soon, the jagged glass of the towering Shard building came into sight, the glass changing colour every few moments from red to green and back again. Moving on, I saw the river appear, its bridges empty and unlit. I was floating westward in the warm air towards Lambeth Palace and the garden.

Higher and higher I went, and looking down I saw there was more than one Lambeth Palace. There were dozens of them along the river bank, tiny versions like toys, with moonlit gardens wrapping around the dark buildings, all more or less the same but not exactly the same. Everything was far below but it was still possible to make out a labyrinth in each garden, cut into the luminous grass but too small and too distant to trace the routes of the spiral pathways.

There was nobody around, nothing to disturb the night. I tried to go slowly down and visit those gardens, but found I could not. Eventually, I must have turned over in my sleep and left all of those dreams as the millions of other sleepers across London slumbered on and on and dreamed their own dreams.

SUMMER GLADES

Today is 21 June, the summer solstice. It is the longest day of the year, followed by the shortest night, traditionally a time for many different festivals across various parts of the northern hemisphere. Midsummer's Day is a day of celebration, and one significant ritual on this day is to eat the first strawberries of the season. There are none of the bigger garden hybrid strawberries growing here but there are plenty of the smaller wild ones, so I will go and search for a handful or two later on.

It is a warm afternoon and I am making my way to a newly planted area to take a closer look at how things are getting on there. Summer is sometimes called the sweet season, the months when so much seems to be in bud and bloom. The air is maybe a little too hot but then a few clouds appear from nowhere to cover the sun, causing everything to dim and cool. Up above, a white aeroplane cuts its way across the sky.

As I turn the corner, the new planting opens up before me, a glorious sea of colour in red, blue and pink, wave after wave shimmering in the summer light. Only a year ago, a large and scruffy box hedge occupied this area but it came under attack from box tree caterpillars, a fairly new intruder to our gardens. They chewed away the foliage at an astonishing rate until eventually the whole hedge was practically destroyed. It is quite unusual for a caterpillar to devastate its only host plant in this manner.

Rather than replanting the box and repeating the whole process, a new opportunity was opened up by the caterpillars' destruction of the hedge. A chance was presented to create something new for the garden by taking a different direction. So, I came up with a plan for the small team of gardeners and volunteers to work on, beginning with digging up the dead plants that had been wrecked by the caterpillars and shredding the stems and foliage for mulch.

We put several tons of homemade compost over the area we had cleared. Next came the planting, usually the thing to look forward to the most in garden projects. In this case, the planting was intended to be an ongoing activity and hopefully will always be ongoing, never reaching a final conclusion but adapting and evolving through the coming years.

I named the new area the Glades, and there can be no denying that this summer it has already come into its own, different from week to week, changing from hour to hour almost. Here, on this Midsummer's Day, it feels as if I am wandering through a free-flowing meadow of wild flowers while strolling through the plantings.

But these are not English wild flowers. They are herbaceous perennials with their origins further afield. Their flowering season is later and much longer than their wilder native counterparts and these perennials should keep going for months, instead of the few weeks that a true English wild meadow would be in bloom.

As winter comes, the Glades will begin to look more and more ramshackle with the plants starting to die back and go over. I will wait until spring before cutting anything back. It may look a bit unkempt for a month or two, but the seeds and dying organic material will offer all kinds of interest for the garden's hungry birds and other wild creatures sharing the space with us, including the many invertebrates and insects. The Glades will provide food as well as plenty of places to shelter.

After the cutting back takes place, any seedlings found can be moved to more convenient places where there are gaps. Most of the perennials can be divided with a spade or fork to make new plants. Many of the cultivars and varieties were chosen in part because they would be suitable for division, allowing more and more new plants to be made for very little effort and no cost. Where patches of ground are a bit empty, these newly divided plants can be moved to fill the gaps and they should prevent any unwanted weeds from taking hold.

So that's how it should work. But where did the idea of a planting like this come from in the first place? It is often said that gardens need new ideas to keep them alive, even a garden such as this one that has been cultivated without interruption for more than 1,000 years. If there is never any new energy, a garden can quickly become stuck; the plantings and even the air can seem rather stale and that affects everything, plants and people alike. Somehow, even the colours seem to fade.

If fresh ideas are needed, where are they to be found? Often gardeners look to other gardens and take inspiration there, study the plants and the different combinations to revise and adapt them on returning to home. That can often work out well, although it can also lead to a repetition of ideas, and too much repetition with the same ideas recycled over and over can stifle the joy from gardening.

While working for the National Trust some years ago, I attended a training course in Ryton run by the Henry Doubleday Research Association on the subject of organic methods. The week of talks and seminars was introduced by our gardens advisor, Bill Malecki, who began by saying:

> Most of us start in our profession because we have grown up with a keen interest in nature. It seems wrong that we then go on to spend the majority of our working lives trying to control and subdue nature, moving further and further away from what drew us to work in gardens in the first place.

That was over fifteen years ago, but Bill's words still ring true and some of the things we went on to look at and consider over that week in Ryton have helped me many times throughout my working life.

Perhaps, then, it should not be surprising that when trying to come up with something new for a garden, I have often found inspiration by placing myself in a setting of wilder nature, maybe in a woodland, meadow or glen where I can closely observe my surroundings and consider how those observations might be developed in a garden.

The possibilities seem endless when wandering through those wild places. The senses are heightened as if hidden instincts are coming back to life again. In those woodlands or meadows, however big or small, I see thousands of plants flowing free across the ground, each with their own unique rhythm and movement in ever-changing combinations – so many combinations and changes that they could never be fully organised, never fully controlled.

On my living room wall at home there is a picture in a frame, a print of *Long Grass and Butterflies* by Vincent van Gogh. It is not an especially good reproduction, much too flat and dull, whereas the original is full of energy, with so much spirit that the paint seems to be lifting right up from the canvas. This magnificent painting can be seen for free by anyone who wishes to if they are able to get to central London. It is in Room 43 of the National Gallery, only about ten minutes' walk from where I am now standing surrounded by the flowers of the Glades on this summer day at Lambeth Palace.

Van Gogh painted the picture in 1890, one of more than 100 he completed in the last six months of his life. Through those intense days and nights, he returned again and again to nature as a subject: flowers and gardens, meadows and trees or swaying fields of ripening wheat. In the hours before his death, he was believed to be working on *Tree Roots*, his last composition. He wrote that these paintings expressed his 'sadness and extreme loneliness' but also the hope that 'the canvasses will tell you what I cannot say in words'.

The pictures van Gogh made of gardens are often referred to as showing areas that had become overgrown and wild, places where once there was order and balance but somehow that balance had been lost through inattention or lack of time, or possibly because of something else. That might well be true. But without question, this series of last paintings also capture the sheer energy of plant life in all its wonder, the constant motion and forming of patterns, colours and shapes that come and go in surprising ways, both complex and beautiful. There may be a sort of chaos to these compositions, although as you look closer, they always seem to make sense on their own terms in the end. He was an artist with a highly tuned sensitivity for plants and plant life.

So, when thinking about the open space that had opened up with the ruined box hedge removed, that painting, *Long Grass and Butterflies*, came to my mind – the thought of a garden area where nature could run free. First, I had to choose the plants – ten or eleven different kinds of herbaceous perennials to begin with.

Some salvias would be essential. I would like to have rudbeckias and echinacea as well, then tannas and penstemons. In no time, I had too many choices, so much to consider. The rule I made for myself was to stay within ten or so plant types that would associate well, to give a coherence to the planting as a whole; the same kind of coherence I witness in nature. Some annuals would be good for this new planting to add an extra element of surprise, because they are likely to appear wherever they feel like appearing, often in chance places, making unforeseen combinations with the other plants. Each year, I collect the seeds from various annuals and keep them in envelopes to be scattered later on, my particular favourites being calendula, nigella, larkspur and snapdragon, among many others. I could go on and on.

The principles of planned accidents are in play here – rhythm, movement, ever-changing patterns, random colours and textures. The kinds of things that are shown so vividly in that Vincent van Gogh painting *Long Grass and Butterflies.* I am sort of in control of this herbaceous meadow but I must try to let go of things in some ways, if any of it is going to work out.

Although the planting plan started out with some clear ideas and principles, hopefully it has not become fixed on any of those. Instead, this kind of garden never arrives but just keeps going, changing from month to month and year to year, moving away from predetermined outcomes.

And once again, the potential for dialogue is open; the exchange between garden and gardener can take place without either trying to domineer. Over the years, I have learned to gladly accept the poppies, foxgloves, wild dianthus or whatever else shows up unannounced, even though none of them were in my plans. They all came from the garden itself, from seeds floating through the air or hidden in the compost. From time to time, I will have to intervene. I will have to stand my ground to make my opinions and wishes known. But I also have to recognise that a change of mind is always possible. Ideas can be adjusted, new impulses accommodated, and little by little, or maybe even quite quickly, I can accept less control and just let the garden be.

The midsummer afternoon is coming to an end and I am on my knees with a hand fork, taking out a few stray weeds that have found their way into the path – bits of grass mostly, with some vetch and clover as well. As I work, the tall trees stand around me taking in the scene. The sun will set slowly today, as it always does on the day of the solstice, but I can see the shadows around me are already lengthening.

I look up as a beam of golden sun comes through the green leaves to catch hundreds of insects floating in the light. Soon it will be time for me to go, to take my bucket and empty it onto the compost heap. But I will wait here for a minute, listening to the songs of the blackbirds and robins, then take my things and slowly leave the midsummer garden.

LONG GRASS

Moving into July and most of the grass in the garden is much longer than usual. For various different reasons, there just has not been enough time for mowing this year; not as much as before. But this has brought several significant benefits as the shaggier grass has allowed many kinds of summer wild flowers to come through where the lawns have overgrown – if overgrown is the right word.

Near the greenhouse, there is a patch of pale gold flowers under the apple trees, a low sweep of Galium verum, which is often described as a common lawn weed, something some might consider a nuisance that spoils the perfect finish of a flat grass surface. It is early morning and I am pausing for a few moments here, beside the greenhouse, standing under the apple trees to admire the Galium and look more closely at those small wands of golden flowers.

This apparent weed would certainly have been present in this garden throughout the centuries, back to medieval times and beyond. Its aromatic foliage would have been cut and allowed to dry by the gardeners and then, when ready, the plant material would have been placed inside mattresses and bedding as a means of repelling fleas, quite a common problem in London back then. Often overlooked these days, the modest Galium verum would have served an extremely useful role in helping the Lambeth Palace residents, both high and humble, to rest peacefully at night, undisturbed by the bites of fleas and so arrive better prepared for the duties of the following day.

It is a twentieth-century thing, the concept of an ideal lawn always cut to a precise height, sometimes even measured by laser to the millimetre, with a velvety surface that must be an unreal and consistent shade of deep green throughout. There can be no weeds, no flowers – and I have to say, that seems like a shame. As I walk further into the garden this morning, I see there are fresh daisies and buttercups pushing through where the grass is longer, pale blue speedwell and golden trefoil close to the ground. There are purple knapweeds as well. It lifts the spirits to see them all.

These longer grass areas tend to be dense and moist at the base where there is shelter from the sun and wind, and that provides a habitat for different creatures. This summer I have heard the songs of thousands of grasshoppers. I don't remember hearing them here before, although I could be mistaken. They are part of an ancient group of insects that were around on earth more than 250 million years ago. I wonder how they sensed there was something for them in this particular garden over the high wall. I wonder what brought them here, where they had not been before, somehow realising so quickly that we have much more long-grass habitat than in previous years. Their song is quite loud today, a humming vibration filling the warm air.

Then there are the butterflies to think about. Species such as heaths, skippers and small coppers all rely on long grass for food from the flowers and as a place for laying their eggs. If we keep cutting the grass down, those butterflies would never be given a chance.

Most gardens are quite small, much smaller than this walled garden of 10 acres. In a smaller space, there may not be much of a lawn, but it is still possible to have a patch of longer grass, even if quite confined. It could be a square metre, or a circle, a triangle, whatever shape appeals. I would think of it as a green pond where there might not be any water but otherwise is a place full of opportunity, a big, wide world for a tiny creature. That dry pond could also provide seeds and pollen for insects and birds.

Whatever the size and shape, it would be best not to mow for as long as possible. When the time comes in the autumn, it would be worth considering using a scythe or shears for cutting – much less damaging, and an activity that is quite enjoyable, surprisingly enough. Various wild creatures that might be hidden in the grass, such as toads, shrews, dormice or beetles, would be in less danger if they were no longer confronted by a noisy mechanical mower with whirling blades.

When I was a gardener at Overbecks in Devon for the National Trust, we bought scythes for the garden, learned how to use them and took care of all our long grass in that way. It was hard work but we loved it.

This July day has gone quickly by and is coming to an end. I'm thinking of giving the bike a rest, perhaps leaving it leant against the wall by the shed and making my way home through the summer evening on foot.

Instead of going the usual way through the back streets, there is another route along the river embankment, heading east, and I set off in that direction. After nearly 2 miles walking along beside the water, I am nearly at the halfway point of the journey, which is at London Bridge. There are not too many people about on the embankment but plenty of cars on the roads.

Eventually, the familiar shape of the bridge I am looking for appears ahead, but before reaching it, I turn into the covered area of Borough Market alongside. Everything is unusually still and dark in there because all of the stalls are now shut up and closed. Dust floats in the air and a few pages of crumpled newspaper blow around at my feet, the newsprint by now too old to be readable.

There has been a market of some kind in this exact location for at least 1,000 years, perhaps even longer, according to some. A faraway voice rings around the empty space, echoing up to the vaulted roof where there are many windows. I might have expected them to be spattered and stained with the city's grime, but they are surprisingly clean.

Pausing there with the deserted market all around, I can hear the constant hum of traffic in the background, going to and from London Bridge. When the Romans created *Londinium*, they built a pontoon crossing made of timber at this point of the Thames to take advantage of the natural ford, which had been the usual way to traverse the stretch of water for those without a boat.

In the midst of Borough Market's growing sprawl, Southwark Cathedral can be found, surrounded by the swirl of commerce but still standing a little apart. It is below the level of the road to the bridge and looks as if it were slightly submerged. There have been Christian worshippers living on this site for a long time, some records suggesting that a community of nuns was established here as early as the seventh century. A minster is mentioned in the 1086 Domesday Book, and this minster eventually became a parish church known as St Saviour's. By the 1800s, it had fallen into serious disrepair and there were suggestions that it should be demolished to accommodate the new plans for the building of a bigger and better London Bridge. Angry arguments about the project went back and forth for many years. Eventually, rather than demolish the church, the decision was made to restore it instead. Deemed too large to continue as a parish church, there were moves to have it converted into a cathedral, and that eventually happened in 1905.

This evening, standing in the centre of the cathedral, looking around and watching the light angle through the windows to trace strange ghostly patterns across the walls, maybe it would not be apparent at first that the building forms the shape of a cross, the long nave running straight through the middle as the central line, with an arm to each side created by the transepts. Many cathedrals, abbeys and churches are laid out in this cruciform design. Someone once told me the reason for building this way was so that any angel passing above would know from the shape of the cross below that they were moving over sacred ground, and if needed, they could use these cruciform patterns to guide them on their journeys.

Moving back outside, I am thinking of the garden I just left at Lambeth as it must be now, in the slowly fading evening with the sun softening. I am picturing that light falling where the grass has been allowed to grow longer in the large lawn area beyond the raised terrace, the area that is sometimes known as the Back Field. For many years, this area had been cut every week without fail, one of the gardeners going up and down with a mower in a fairly relentless way. It is quite tedious to do, a waste of fuel and maybe also a waste of time to keep mowing routinely such a large expanse so frequently. It would take several hours to complete, with the added drawback that the close-cut finished lawn was fairly dull to look at and provided little if anything by way of habitat for the garden's wilder inhabitants.

Wishing to make a change, when considering the options for the area I thought about Southwark Cathedral and other churches, I thought about the shape of the cross that was evident when observed from above. So, I let all the grass grow and mowed paths through it, two paths to form a living cross, trying to replicate the same cruciform pattern of those churches. To provide the new structure with some clarity and a frame, I cut the grass shorter around the whole thing. It ended up as a kind of installation on quite a big scale, providing an impressive space for a lot of long grass – a whole new grass meadow, as it turned out.

The focal point of all this was intended to be the labyrinth, which is found in the place where the altar would be at the top of the long, green path representing the nave. The labyrinth is also the focal point of the garden as a whole, a still point in the ever-turning world, a place at the centre of everything that allows time for quiet reflection and prayer. The circular shape emphasises the equality of all as they pray and worship in their different ways. It can be difficult to make a clear link between the history of a site and the garden it contains, but by organising the long grass in that way I hoped to make a strong connection between the garden and Lambeth Palace as a centuries-old site for prayer.

Even in the space of a year, I have seen how these unshaded areas of meadow have allowed a much more diverse range of wild creatures to be observed as they find more of what they need here, be they butterflies, grasshoppers, moths, bees or dragonflies. Hopefully, this new meadow can become a haven for different communities of wildlife, and if the areas are managed well, only cutting the grass once and at the right time which, for here, most years would probably be around August, then those wild creatures living with us would have a good chance to complete their natural cycles.

In the evening, the meadow grass sways in the breeze, all rusty brown, gold and purple. A group of starlings suddenly appear, dozens of them swooping down to see what they might find in this inviting terrain. The grass field must resemble, in a distant way, the fields of wheat and barley that were once grown in these grounds, fields that provided the grain to make the bread to feed those living here.

But maybe that is enough for the time being. I don't know if I am supposed to be standing in the palace garden surrounded by long grass or if I am still somewhere in the shadows between Southwark Cathedral and Borough Market. I imagine it is the latter. I should leave the empty market place behind and head home before it gets too late, I am only halfway back and I'm tired, my feet are tired. Now I wish I had brought my bike with me after all.

Crossing the busy street and heading towards Guy's Hospital, I wander on through Bermondsey as far as the Old Kent Road, then cross that busy thoroughfare full of noise and speed, until at last I can go into the green of Burgess Park. Almost at once, I see the vast lake where the water birds live. I see the imperious cormorants standing with wings extended on top of various small, floating platforms. It is an extraordinary park. It was only created in the 1980s, but is well planned and well looked after, with plenty of areas where wilder plants are allowed to grow in peace.

The air feels much fresher now. It has been a long walk but I am nearly home.

Since May this year, Southwark Council has instigated a new approach to mowing across the borough, which includes this park – cutting a third less grass than in previous years. Just as at Lambeth Palace, this has allowed the flowering plants that had long been suppressed by the mower's blades to come through, as well as permitting millions of flower seeds to germinate; seeds that may have been lying dormant for many years on the surface of the soil, where they were only waiting for a small chance to get going. The park management said that they had been wanting to see what would come up, and it had been much more diverse than could have been expected or hoped for. As a footnote, they added that if they had decided on such a course of action five years ago, their inboxes would have been jammed with complaints about the uncut long grass. But not now – some proof that things are changing.

Since the 1930s, more than 97 per cent of the meadow lands across the UK have been lost. But hopefully there can now be a concerted effort by all of us responsible for the management of grass areas to try to return at least some of that valuable habitat to meadow, just by organising mowing in different ways. If that were to happen, then some of what has been lost might be regained.

FLIGHT

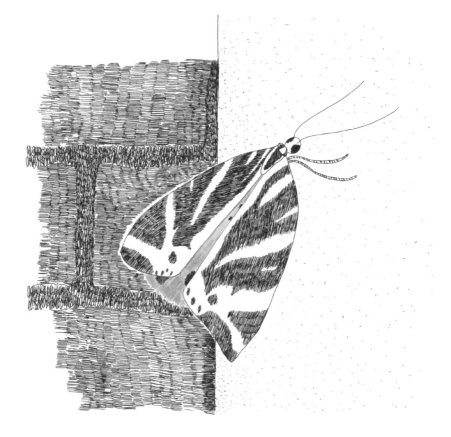

nother warm day in July and I am to be found once again, wheeling my wheelbarrow between the avenues of olives on the wide gravel path behind the palace. To my left, there comes a sudden burst of very loud bird song. Looking towards the sound, I can see a sparrow with chest puffed out and eyes fixed upward, singing as loud as he or she can towards the sunlit sky. The little bird is perched 10ft up in the air at the apex point of one of the topiary yew pyramids that line the path, trilling at top voice.

For the last few weeks, I have been hearing the burbling of young birds coming from inside the dense cover provided by those green pyramids but wasn't quite sure what it was. Last year, several blackbirds made nests in there; this year, it seems to have been the turn of the sparrows.

In the 1970s, they were recorded as the most common species in England, estimated to number more than 25 million. Sparrows were everywhere. Unfortunately, these days, their appearances are scarcer and they now feature on the RSPB's red list for endangered birds. Soon they may only be occasional visitors to our gardens, scrabbling around for scraps where they can find them, these small songbirds with their elegant plumage of brown and pale grey. They need more places to build their nests, and evergreen hedges are a favoured location for them. It is not so surprising, then, that the sparrow serenading so loudly today chose to build a home inside that pyramid of clipped yew.

Turning away from the green topiary to face the open lawn, I look over at the raised terrace on the opposite side, an elevated area like a thin stage, long and narrow, as it runs from east to west, parallel to the path where I am standing. Just beyond the terrace, there is another parallel line made by a hedge of pleached limes. There are fifty-one trees altogether in that hedge, and they create a kind of living screen, which is useful because it prevents the entire garden being viewed in one go, allowing at least a little of its mystery and surprise to be retained.

Pleached hedges are usually created by planting dozens of trees such as hornbeams or limes quite close together at even distances in a straight line. They are clipped so that when in leaf they appear to be a continuous green, sculpted block with the straight trunks coming down from the foliage at even intervals like a troop of soldiers standing to attention. It is all artifice and effect, but when shaped well, these hedges can make quite an impression. The earliest records of this kind of pleaching being done in London date from 1324, so it is a garden practice with a long history.

Each February and March at Lambeth Palace, the tall ladder must be brought out to complete the pruning work on that long row of lime trees. It is easy enough but takes several weeks to do. I have to stretch across from the top of the ladder with secateurs in hand, carefully cutting away the new branches of the limes. They are of varying shades from yellow to orange to red, lighting up in bright colours on cold winter afternoons when caught by the occasional low, slanting rays of sunlight breaking through the grey clouds above the palace.

Earlier this year, while carrying out this pleaching task, I was joined by a small patrol of long-tailed tits, twenty or so of them. They trundled slowly along the top of the hedge in a loose formation, picking off any aphids revealed by the pruning I had done. Murmuring and chattering quietly to each other, they eventually came very close to where I was working. There, they paused to take a good look at me – interested, but not very interested – showing no inclination to take flight but instead, after a moment or two of hesitation, continuing to gather the aphids without any further concern. Perhaps because I was in an unexpected place, high up on my ladder, they did not identify me as a potential predator.

Those grubs they were after are rich in protein and therefore a vital food source for a bird. Long-tailed tits are not very efficient with seeds or berries, meaning the winters can be long and hard for them, so an early spring gathering of protein-rich aphids is valuable. They seem to be finding enough in the garden to keep them going and we have made sure there are good places for them to peacefully make their elaborate nests, if they wish to, and have noticed several of those beautiful constructions in various of our hedges over the last few years.

While the long-tailed tits may not obtain too much from seeds or berries, these are an essential food for many of the other garden birds living with us. Some plants, like fennel or verbena, hold their ripened seeds for a quite a while after flowering and that can be especially helpful for the smaller birds, who can balance on the slender stems to collect what they need. Robins, wrens and sparrows benefit from this, while bigger rivals such as the menacing crows can only observe proceedings from a distance, knowing they are far too heavy to perch on those thin branches without collapsing the whole thing.

Many years ago, when starting out on a life as a gardener with the National Trust in Devon, I was met on my first day by the estate manager who said, 'There are three things we've got for you. First, your dark blue uniform, always to be worn when on duty so the visitors know who you are. Second, your set of hand tools, take good care of them. And third and final, you'll find your own personal robin will be waiting for you somewhere out in the garden.'

I had two robins with me most days for the ten years I was there. They became so familiar that they would often land on my shoe or even on my shoulder as I was working.

The longest recorded lifespan for a robin is nineteen years, although on average they only live about twelve months. They can be aggressive to each other and will defend a set territory with fierce tenacity, and this is exactly what dozens of robins are doing around here in the garden right now in the height of summer.

Part of the territorial behaviour involves making their presence known to others by singing at top volume, which is pretty loud considering how small they are. They tend to keep up the singing through all the seasons, their sweet melodies often the only birdsong to be heard through the darker days of the cold winter months.

Much as I like robins, I have to admit that my favourite singers of all are the blackbirds, with their endless, flowing tunes, forever finding some new and inventive twist for their weird melodies. It has been good to note a big rise in the number of them in the garden this year, along with their relative, the song thrush. Early yesterday, I was walking through the Glades, watching as the morning light caught them in full flower. No doubt disturbed by my presence, suddenly around twenty song thrushes flew up into the air from beneath the plantings to wait in the branches of some nearby trees. Once I had passed by and was far enough away, they returned from the trees to their scavenging for food beneath the plants. I was glad to have seen this happen, glad to have been up and about so early in the day.

Blackbirds have a preference for the open ground of a lawn or something similar as they hunt for food, their heads on one side as they listen carefully for the movement of any earthworms before suddenly pouncing. In the shadier corners, they find an array of rewards under the fallen leaves. Over the last year or two, I have seen that they have learnt a new trick. In the autumn, they suspend themselves upside down beneath the clusters of bright red berries that cover the rowan trees, holding on with their talons while they spread their wings for balance. It is a strange sight, a little awkward and ungainly, but from that position they can get at the fruit. Their determination has to be admired.

Those rowan trees are planted in an informal avenue near the Glades and are also of interest to those song thrushes I interrupted when I walked by earlier. They go through the trees one by one as if they have an agreed system, finishing the berries from one tree before even starting on the next, methodical and exact. They seem to be a bit less heavy than the blackbirds and can gather the fruits without the need for any awkward acrobatics. I saw as many as ten of them working together at the same time on one small tree.

The garden has been quiet this summer, with few people around, and various of the smaller songbird inhabitants have been able to make the most of the calm. And the numbers of butterflies living with us have also increased. There are about seventy-one species of butterfly regularly observed in England and so far I have seen around twenty of those species in the garden, which is not too bad a number. No sign of the elusive Camberwell beauty yet, but maybe soon. I still have hope. Camberwell Green is only just down the road, so I expect one or two will turn up here one day, unless their name is misleading and they are not local to Camberwell at all.

Butterflies are thought to have evolved from moths. There are many more species of moth – around 160,000. They are often dismissed as drab little things that flit about at night, sometimes coming indoors to make holes in favourite carpets or finding ways into a wardrobe to cause various kinds of trouble. But there is more to consider. Moths have got a lot going on in general, and are vital to a healthy ecosystem, carrying out crucial pollination of various flowering plants. Humans would struggle to survive without the pollinating moths going about their nocturnal activities, moving around in silence and mostly unseen by any of us. Their caterpillars also provide a nutritious food source for many birds and other wild creatures. Unfortunate for the moth perhaps, but that's the way it is, out there in the wild.

We had a special visitor last week, Stephen, who is a great expert on moths. He came in to join us early in the morning before he set off for work in the centre of town. As he rested his bike against the wall, the first thing he noticed was a large tiger moth poised on the drainpipe outside Comfort's house. We saw several of these last year, but this summer there have been even more sightings. With their precise black and white outer wings and pale orange inner body, they look exotic, like some beautiful immigrant that has blown in on a warm air current from the south. Those looks are deceiving, for they are defined as a native species, although, according to Butterfly Conservation, they have been in steady decline in England for the last fifty years. The loss of trees, hedgerows and other essential plants due to building developments are to blame.

Stephen has been very generous to us in helping survey and identify the various moths we have in the garden. His enthusiasm and knowledge are an inspiration. He points out that monitoring our moth population will give us a useful indicator of the general changes in the garden's ecology. With Alice, he and I spent a fascinating hour, first thing last Friday morning, checking what had been attracted overnight into the moth trap that he bought for us a little while ago. The moths are drawn towards the trap's bright light, possibly mistaking it for a strange flower or even the moon.

When I was 5 or 6, I remember seeing moths around the outdoor lights and being told that they were trying to fly to the moon. Another theory is that moths find their way around by sensing the angle of a distant source of light, for example, the stars, or possibly the moon again, and they adjust their flight tracks to keep that angle of light as constant as possible. This is called transverse orientation. I don't know – the theory is difficult to follow.

I have often noticed that moths are attracted to the paler flowers in the garden, particularly those with a strong scent, regardless of where the moon or stars might be. And then they fly in a complex series of jagged spirals and loops. Surely it would be impossible for them to keep the angle of distant light fixed and constant – the moonlight or the starlight – when they are flying along such crooked lines.

On opening the moth trap, we found there were 160 specimens inside, which surpassed all our moth count records. It is still not that many, but it is good to see the numbers increasing, as last year our highest count was forty-one. Many of our finds were micro-moths, very small creatures that might not be noticed unless you are looking very closely.

There were also dozens of heart and darts, footmen and a few emeralds. Some angle shades were there, along with a tussock or two, a square spot rustic and possibly a tree lichen beauty. I am hoping to see a pebble hooktip some misty morning.

Nothing is harmed in carrying out these moth surveys. The insects rest in the trap, where they keep still for a few hours among the empty cardboard egg boxes we have placed there for them the evening before. Each moth is counted and named, if it can be identified, and while doing so, we have to be careful not to touch the wings where the scales overlap like so many tiny, coloured roof tiles. Those scales are fragile and can disintegrate to dust very easily on contact with clumsy human fingers.

When their presence has been recorded, the moths are released uninjured early in the morning, after what was hopefully no more than a slightly confusing episode for them.

GROWING PRODUCE

When the first version of Lambeth Palace was built on the banks of the Thames more than 800 years ago, the site was chosen in part because it already had a productive garden, which was organised and managed by the Benedictine monks from Rochester, who had been gardening here for more than a century, from at least 1066 onwards. There was good reason to be confident that the newly acquired garden would provide enough fruit, vegetables and herbs to sustain the new community that was intending to take up residence once the new palace was built to house them.

There was the wide river running by alongside, providing a ready source of fresh water close at hand, and the terrain was reasonably flat, although marshy. The open aspect of the land offered plenty of light and must have been ideal for growing all kinds of produce.

Large ponds were probably already there, having been installed by the monks. If not, new ones would have been dug out and lined with puddled clay, making a place where fish could multiply and be easily caught when needed for food, especially on significant occasions such as saints' days. The kinds of fish found in those ponds is unknown but most likely bream or perch would have been present. The monks' diet was mostly vegetarian, with plenty of green vegetables and fruit when available. Cereals were a staple mainstay of each day, usually in the form of grainy bread or a thick porridge.

After completing the construction of Lambeth Palace, a dairy was built to house the community's herd of cows. When the Museum of London's archaeological team came to the garden in 2017 to make some excavations in one place, a couple of metres down, they uncovered the preserved skeleton of a cow carefully laid out on its side as if resting peacefully. Clay tobacco pipes unearthed nearby suggested the skeleton could be from the 1700s. As I looked down into the fresh pit, I wondered why this animal had been buried in such a way; why its body had been so carefully and neatly arranged. Perhaps the death had been from an illness or disease and separation from the rest of the herd was necessary. Or maybe she had been a favourite of the Lambeth Palace community and therefore had been laid to rest with delicate ceremony.

As well as the dairy, we know that there was also a bakery within the grounds and a mill for milling flour to make the bread and other foodstuffs. The gardeners grew fields of wheat and barley to supply the grain, while the mills' grindstones were powered by water diverted from the Thames and fed into a narrow channel that ran across the garden.

The river water flowing through the garden must have been quite a sight. The channel might still be there. It has probably run dry by now but could still be intact, I suspect, beneath the raised terrace that, according to the pre-1750 maps, was built along the same line west to east that the water channel once traversed.

Some of those maps also show that the garden space was laid out in a geometric system of small, raised beds linked by brick paths. These would have been filled with edibles, mostly different sorts of vegetables and salads.

The palace's orchards are indicated a little further away from the main building, towards the east side. It must have been quite a feeling back then to walk through the garden on an early August day like this one, surrounded by such abundance. The structures of that older garden may well still be hidden beneath the present garden, covered by thousands of tons of good soil brought in from elsewhere and screed over the top.

I wonder if the monastic garden is waiting silently down there and slowly breaking apart with the natural movement of the ground. After the longer spells of weather without rain, sometimes a few ghostly shapes and outlines of the older garden start to appear where the lawns are dry and baked. I wonder if someday someone will be allowed to excavate just a little, to try to find the remains of those buried gardens.

These days, if fruit and vegetables are to be grown at Lambeth Palace it must be done in the margins to leave the centre as open lawn. This is to allow the garden space to be used for public occasions – parties, big-scale staged concerts and so on. Those areas where the gardeners would like to grow fruit and vegetables are not available and the planting tends to be pushed out to the edges of the site, where various mature trees are located, some of them more than 250 years old. The shade from these big trees, along with a lack of moisture under them, makes growing produce of good quality quite difficult.

We would probably have to go back some eighty years to find a truly productive garden here, to the time of the Second World War when Lambeth Palace gave its grounds over to allotments as part of the Dig for Victory campaign that was launched in 1941. Many green spaces all over the country were involved, even the lawns outside the Tower of London were converted into vegetable plots.

These days, we are seeing something similar happening as open or largely derelict urban areas are being explored as potential sites for growing produce. This has been particularly evident with the success of the Incredible Edible movement, which was started in Yorkshire in 2008, steadily gaining momentum all around the world as similar groups have set up along similar lines. It has been a positive way to provide edible produce from unlikely places while looking to address some of the questions regarding the way our food is produced and transported. Incredible Edible aims to keep communities closer together by enabling people to garden together.

Back in 1941, the aims of the Dig for Victory campaign were not so different. The idea was not only to provide vital self-grown food but also to strengthen solidarity as communities tried to cope with the immense strain of war, and through gardening, civilian morale was supported and encouraged during some dark times. There are several powerful images of people growing things back then. Recently, I even saw a photograph of an elegantly dressed woman watering plants with a watering can while surrounded by rubble after a devastating Blitz bombing. I could not find any pictures of the allotment gardens at Lambeth Palace, so what they were like can only be imagined.

One thing those wartime gardeners could not have known is that digging the soil has some surprising health benefits. Working with a fork and spade in ground that has been well composted releases geosmin molecules. Their presence is identified by the distinctive musty smell that becomes apparent as the earth is moved. These invisible organic compounds are ingested while breathing, the aroma from these beneficial molecules is something like the smell that rises from dry ground after rainfall.

The health benefits of geosmin were first identified by the oncologist Dr Mary O'Brien towards the beginning of this century, while treating patients with lung cancer at the Royal Marsden Hospital in South Kensington, not too far from where I am working in the garden today, on the other side of the river. Since those initial findings, further research has shown that the body ingesting geosmin through breathing allows serotonin to be released into our systems, which can counter depression and bring an overall feeling of well-being, even helping to strengthen immune systems.

But today is high summer in the garden and there will be no digging. If only it would rain, the water drops hitting the ground would cause geosmin molecules to be released into the air. Looking around on this warm August afternoon, everything seems too dry; the downpours of June are just a memory. July has passed with no rain and this month has been much the same so far. The garden could do with some rainfall.

Somehow, the trees all look fine. They must be pulling up gallons of water to keep themselves going from somewhere much further down, far below the sun-baked surface. Maybe the River Thames is moving underneath the garden much more than I realise.

Walking on towards the Chapel Garden to check on the herbs, I can see that some of the plants here are enjoying the hot, dry weather. The rosemary, sage and thyme are all thriving as if they were back in the Mediterranean, their land of origin. Among them, some intruders have appeared, with no intention of discreetly hiding but instead revealing themselves with fanfares of soft yellow flowers that are impossible to miss. These are evening primroses, but how they got into the herb garden is a mystery. Perhaps a passing bird dropped the seeds by mistake.

A native of North America, these plants first began to be grown in Europe from the early seventeenth century onwards, although for a long time, nobody seemed to be aware of their potential both for medicine and for the kitchen. Every part is edible, even the roots can be eaten raw. As a remedy, evening primrose has also been used to alleviate various skin ailments and some believe it may reduce high blood pressure, while helping with other heart conditions. I have to smile at least a little to see that it has somehow placed itself right there, in exactly the place it should be, in the Chapel Garden surrounded by all kinds of other medicinal and kitchen herbs.

Although it has been warm again today, the temperature is beginning to fall quite quickly as the afternoon goes by, so maybe the rain will come tonight after all. A few rumbles of distant thunder were heard a little earlier but none of that has amounted to anything so far, although a change is definitely in the air and that would be a good thing.

The herbs around me continue to bask in the heat and at least we still have a suitable place to grow these valuable plants. There are a few apple and pear trees to the edges of this part of the garden, trained espalier style and tied to the red railings. From the first day of the garden's beginnings, all those centuries ago, choosing and planting fruit trees would have been a key element of the gardener's role here. The garden staff had to have the skills and experience to take action at different times of the year to allow the orchards to succeed.

Other than the ones I am looking at here in the herb garden, there are very few fruit trees growing in the grounds now, following the general trend in England where 90 per cent of traditional orchards have been lost since the 1950s. Of those that remain, half are said to be in a very poor state. Maybe soon there will be none left, and all that rich wildlife habitat will be gone, all that amazing fruit also gone.

Up by the greenhouse, there are a few apple trees as well as a pear and a plum. We also have the old quince; an exceptional tree, with odd knobbly, yellow fruits that cannot be eaten raw but can be prepared in various ways, the best of all being the sweet membrillo that is made in Spain, a dark brown solid jelly often served with slices of strong Manchego cheese.

Quince trees have been in cultivation for a long time. They were being grown for cropping in the Akkadian Empire of Mesopotamia 4,500 years ago. In Europe, they have mostly been confined to the south, which is not so surprising as they can ripen more easily in the warmer climate. But that has not stopped those further north trying to grow them. The first known plantings of quinces in England were carried out at the instruction of Edward I and were sited around the Tower of London in 1275.

In our time, we have seen how climate change has altered our gardens and, in some cases, it has meant that something like a fruiting quince can be easier to grow with the warmer temperatures now. It has also meant that pests and diseases not seen before in our temperate region are on the increase, while the weather has become more extreme in the winter, followed by difficult spells of long drought in the summer months.

A couple of years ago, I bought a big lemon tree from a nursery in Richmond and planted it in an oak barrel near the garden entrance. There is quite a thrill to seeing it just now because the branches are covered with ripening lemons. But at the same time, I am thinking of those places further to the south, places like Barcelona, where I used to work, areas where citrus trees have been grown for centuries and are a traditional part of local economies. Changing weather patterns mean that it is getting too hot and dry to grow the usual produce as effectively as before.

Leaving those worrying thoughts aside for a while, I realise it must be time to find a shady place for an afternoon break, a glass of cool water and something small to eat. An old, slightly broken bench has been left behind the greenhouse where there is a thicket of very sweet raspberries that are ripening nicely just now. The other day, I went to sit on that bench, with the cat coming to join me, and as we rested there in the welcome silence, we were both alerted to a loud, rustling sound that we could hear in the raspberry thicket. Suddenly, a blackbird stumbled out a yard away from us with a large raspberry in his beak – glossy black feathers, shining yellow beak, soft red fruit.

'That's a bit odd,' I thought, and the cat, gazing calmly down at the bird, might well have been thinking much the same. The blackbird finished his sugary snack in his own time and then carefully surveyed the surroundings, maybe listening for something that we couldn't hear while checking he hadn't left any worthwhile scraps on the ground. I looked at the cat and the cat looked at me while the blackbird shook out his shining feathers and flew off over the wall.

Those shining black feathers brought a dream back to me that I had the night before, a simple sort of a dream, I suppose. Standing on the main lawn behind the palace, I was placing twelve stout sticks in the ground to see how a twelve-tree cherry orchard might look if it were planted in the big, empty space there. The sun was shining, and several lingering crows eyed me suspiciously before continuing to tear at the lawn, slowly ruining the smooth, emerald surface with their big beaks as they went in search of the juicy chafer grubs just under the grass.

I prepared the twelfth stick for my new cherry orchard, ready to tap the last stake into the ground with my hammer when, without warning, the back door of the building crashed open and voices began shouting. They were so loud and confused that it was impossible to make any sense of the words. Nobody came out through the door but, at once, the scared crows on the lawn took flight; they scarpered, squawking.

I looked down to the green at my feet and saw that it had turned sable brown, like dry straw, and was strewn with rubble and broken glass. A sharp ray of sunlight caught those broken shards for a moment, sparkling red, blue and green, glittering there for a second or two and then gone an instant later. Everything had quietened down completely, even the constant traffic in the street had hushed. With the twelfth stick still poised in my hand, I heard a squirrel cough politely from a high branch up in the tulip tree.

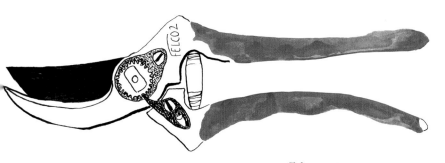

Felco secateurs.

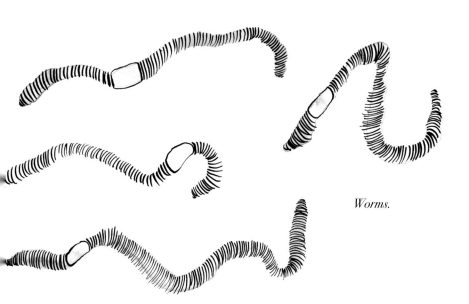

Worms.

Iris.

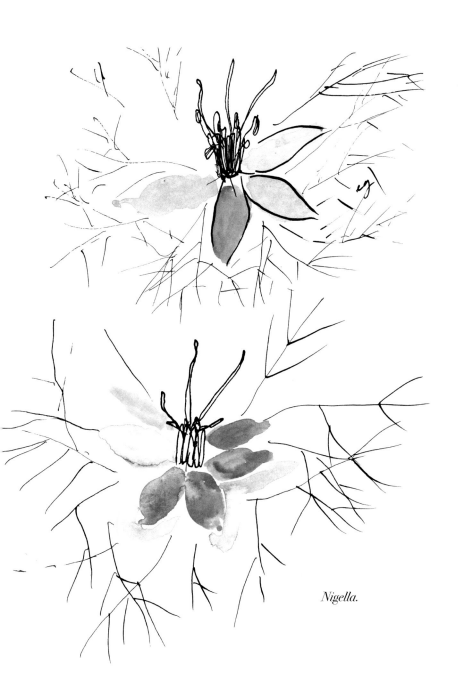

Nigella.

Dreams.

Tiger moths.

Salvia.

Garden arch.

Olives.

Pyramidal orchid.

SCYTHE

This week, a scythe was delivered to the Gatehouse at the entranceway. It came by ordinary post, the curved blade carefully wrapped in heavy brown paper, the object unmistakeable by its shape, with the wooden handle separate alongside also in a thick wrapping of parcel paper.

As I walked under the stone archway, early yesterday morning, I was not expecting anything unusual, but there it was, something new waiting for collection in the darkened alcove of the Gatehouse. An extraordinary day in the history of Lambeth Palace – the object in my hands was the first scythe to be present and ready for use in the garden for more than 100 years at least.

Mowing machines of assorted kinds took their place around 1900 but for the first nine centuries of the garden, and maybe even before that, scythes would have been an essential tool for the staff, not only to keep the grass areas mown but also to harvest the cereal crops in the late summer and autumn. It is close to that time now, and although there are no crops to harvest, there is some long meadow grass to be cut before the days turn too cold and wet.

Among the few records in the library archives that refer directly to the garden, there is an interesting item that has been filed under the heading 'Household Ordinances of Matthew Parker'. He served as archbishop from 1559 to 1575. There are several duties for the palace gardeners described in the handwritten note, including the solemn instruction to 'keep the grass lowe with a scythe'.

Why this precise list of required gardening work, I wonder, why would it be so specific? Perhaps the lawns were not being cut in a way that was deemed satisfactory. Or perhaps the gardeners of that time were questioning some of their duties; maybe too much was being demanded of them. I can imagine the murmurs of rebellion heard around the grounds in the evening air, smoke unfurling from small bonfires burning in the furthest corners of the garden.

Almost certainly, scythes crafted in England in the English style would have been used at Lambeth Palace through all those years. These days, it is not easy to obtain an English scythe because their production came to an end in the 1980s. They went out of favour for being too heavy and tiring to work with, so now the lighter Austrian scythe is generally preferred.

The one that arrived for us today came from Wales but is of Austrian origin. It looks simple enough, a curved steel blade attached at an angle to a long piece of wood with contoured handles. The blade was forged by hand and although it may look basic, at least fifteen separate processes were involved in its preparation. Making these tools is still a highly skilled craft.

The use of scythes across the world goes back a long way, possibly more than 7,000 years. The ancient Greeks and Egyptians had them, and they could be seen in action throughout most parts of the Roman Empire. They have been described as the most significant hand tool in the history of agriculture, their use becoming more and more widespread from the eighth century onwards. Some refer to a 'scythe zone' that includes nearly all of Europe, Russia, the Middle East, the northern parts of Africa, China and India.

Soon after the first settlers arrived in North America, the scythe became a crucial tool in the management of crops there. In Massachusetts, a design patent was registered by Joseph Jenckes in 1665, stating that his improved version was for 'the more speedy cutting of grass'. That American design remained popular for the next 300 years with very few modifications.

Although scything might seem to be an activity from a long-distant past, in our times it continues as a valid working method, even if there are relatively few gardeners or farmers still practising the method. It continues for several different reasons, although an obvious motive would be economic because, for some areas, modern machinery such as tractors and mechanical mowers are too expensive or too difficult to obtain, let alone finding the means to cover the colossal price of a something as big as a combine harvester.

Another issue could be the terrain of the field or meadow to be mown. It could be too steep or too rugged, or just plainly inaccessible by vehicle, and in such situations a scythe is the perfect tool for the task, perhaps the only tool.

As an example of this, consider the highlands of Transylvania. They are rocky, remote places with many sharp inclines and valleys. There, the farmers make up teams with their neighbours to go from field to field at harvest time, spending maybe two or three weeks helping to scythe each other's land. Most evenings as the sun begins to set, a small celebration takes place in the newly mown area. There are things to eat and traditional dancing, no doubt accompanied by sufficient bottles of strong plum wine, Transylvanian moonshine – homemade and not to be found in any shops. They must be careful not to overdo things too much, for they know tomorrow's work will be at least as tough as the session they have just done.

One of the most vivid descriptions ever written of a day's scything occurs in *Anna Karenina* by Leo Tolstoy, first published in book form in 1878. There is a long passage in Part Three, featuring one of the main characters, Konstantine Levin, a free-thinking landowner in his early thirties, a man who is generally awkward in company and struggles with the expected social customs and graces. He decides one evening that he will spend the following day cutting grass with a big group of the peasant workers from his family's estate. Experienced in the techniques of meadow mowing, he even has his own scythe, although he is well aware that he might be somewhat out of practice. Before he sets off in the morning, his brother studies him with wonder, hardly able to believe Konstantine would be able to manage an entire day of such challenging physical labour or would even want to. 'All day?' the brother simply asks.

The workers out in the fields are also doubtful, especially when they see his poor efforts in the beginning. In quiet voices, they make their criticisms heard, mixing them with useful advice as they politely suggest various ways he might do better. It is still early in the morning but almost at once he is tired out and fears he will never keep up with the others. He can see them ahead in the meadow, forty-two of them altogether, he counts, of different sizes and ages working steadily as a team, moving confidently across the land. Titus the mowing master is nearby. It seems he is going especially fast to test Levin in some way.

Eventually, there comes a break as Titus finishes a swathe and, resting his scythe on his shoulder, he walks back through the mown field, carefully placing his feet in the footprints made in the cut grass by his own boots. Levin does the same.

Why do they do this? What difference would it make, the marks of their feet in the cut meadow? Could it be they don't want to mar the neatness of their work in any way? Maybe it is something of the same feeling I would have when I avoid pushing a wheelbarrow over a gravel path that has just been freshly raked, not wanting to spoil the even finish, even though it will soon be marked by many other footprints and tyre tracks.

The day goes on, the sun moves higher and the air turns hotter. Sweat runs down Levin's face and drips from his nose. His shirt is drenched in salty water. But he feels happy, and the only thing shadowing that happiness is the poor quality of his work, which he sees as he looks behind him, the grass cut much too unevenly and left in a bit of a mess. The scything team moves on, and working with them he begins to find a good rhythm, a rhythm of his own, and eventually loses all track of time. He has no idea if hours have gone by as they've worked. It could be many hours. Or perhaps it has only been a few minutes, he doesn't know.

A little later, another small but telling episode occurs as they all take a mid-morning rest. They have come to a natural stop by a stream, where an elderly man offers Levin a rusty tin that has just been filled with warm water. Little green weeds from the stream float on the surface. I may not have much, the older man seems to be suggesting, but what little I have I'll gladly share with you, even if it's only this soupy green water in a bashed-up tin cup. Levin drinks and believes he has never tasted anything nicer. In that moment, there is no young landowner, no elderly peasant, just people working together and sharing what they have, however sparse the offerings. They return to the scything refreshed; their spirits lifted.

> The longer Levin went on mowing, the longer he experienced those moments of oblivion, when his arms no longer seemed to swing the scythe, but it was one with him, his body so conscious and full of life… these were blessed moments.

There are wild creatures to manoeuvre carefully around as the mowing team move through the long grass. There are molehills to be negotiated and even a few quails' nests, recently vacated because the slow approach of the scythes gave the birds enough warning and sufficient time to move away. Bright beetles appear and are briefly examined as they scuttle on the tip of the blade for a moment before being put aside to safety in the stubble. And there are hawks wheeling high up in the sky, high above the cut meadow.

All of that seems a long way from Lambeth Palace as we stand here on a cool September morning. A small group has gathered, just four of us. We only have one scythe for the work. I had only obtained one as I wasn't sure if the others would have any interest in working this way. After all, they might prefer to use a mechanical mower instead; it's not for me to say. Thankfully, it was the other way around. Instead of questioning the whole idea, they asked why there weren't more scythes, then we could all have our own to work with at the same time – a proper mowing team. Ah well, maybe next year.

Looking at the grass to be cut, it was clear that it had grown too long. Sections of it were lying flat after the recent rain and that would make our work much more difficult. Next year, I will have to remember that September might be too late for this annual task, and maybe choose a few days in August for the work instead.

We decided to proceed anyway, and in the end, Alice, Charlie, Cheyenne and I all took turns with the scythe, watching and appraising each other's efforts. There is no denying it was challenging, but in the activity we all found something good.

But if it is so hard and so much effort, why would we go to the trouble of cutting the grass in this way? Why not just get the most powerful mower from the machine shed and have done with it? There may not be clear answers to those questions and there does not have to be an answer to everything, but I think that some of the reasons why we might want to work in the traditional way can be found in the pages from *Anna Karenina* described above. When you are scything a meadow, you are out in the open air, you are in nature with a simple tool, an ancient tool. The many wild creatures and insects living in the grass are unlikely to be harmed by your actions as they undoubtedly would have been had you got a petrol mower out with the blur of its rapid blades slicing and crunching everything before it, accompanied by the deafening engine.

Spared all that, the grasshoppers, toads, beetles, mice and other wild creatures should be able to hop or scurry out of the way with no need to hurry too much. As if to prove the point, after I made my first few passes over the long grass, I hesitated for a few seconds to catch my breath, leaning on the scythe. A tiny brown toadlet, no bigger than a penny, hopped onto the shining metal blade and waited there – a toad in exact miniature, probably sensing the imminent danger and opting for the blade as the place of greatest safety. I carefully put the creature out of harm's way and carried on with the work.

Old memories are reawakened; old impulses rediscovered. As each of us sways in an easy movement with the scythe, keeping the blade at an even height, parallel to the ground, we know we are carrying out the same task with the same technique as hundreds of gardeners have done before us in this very garden over many centuries. Even the crafted tool in my hands is also much the same, the design hardly having changed.

There is the sound as well. The swing and the quiet swish of the blade through the waves of grass, with the ebb and flow of the London traffic somewhere far away, fading into the distance as the birds sing loudly in the nearby trees. The laughter and talk of the others is interrupted now and then by the soft clanking of the scythe every time there is a pause to sharpen the blade with the whetstone. Afterwards, we will get out the rakes and make hay from the mown grass. Haymaking – what a thing to be doing in the middle of twenty-first-century London.

SEPTEMBER WALK

The rain came down hard last night and there was more this morning. As I make my way down the garden path, I am dodging around a few puddles in the gravel. After the long dry weeks, the lawns went pale yellow, but those few hours of overnight rain quickly turned that dead-looking grass to a light green, all full of life again.

Wandering down the Long Walk on the west side of the garden, to the left of the path I see that even the gnarled old plane trees are fairly content with themselves, not complaining about anything for once. The shade is fairly heavy in this area, but to my right there are plenty of shrubs and low-growing plants filling the space and covering the ground beneath the big trees; the kinds of things that can get by without very much direct light. It is dry shade in this area, which I think is one of the most difficult gardening situations, especially in an urban setting where the ground seems to get even more dusty and parched. But looking closer, I can see many of the plants are fine, especially the carpets of epimediums, with their leaves of deep green just touched by russet copper markings.

Turning back to the left side of the long, gravel path, I look at the wide river of low ivy running along the edge, flowing around various Japanese maples here and there; small trees placed in big grey concrete pots that seem to float in that green river. Those matching concrete containers were donated years ago from a project a mile or so away at the South Bank. They were unwanted and discarded at the time but at least they have found a new use for a while in the garden here. The maples growing in them are just beginning to show the first traces of autumn colours in their dissected leaves.

Before I walk into the deeper shade, there is something to see at the beginning of this long path; there is a new bed that I cut into the lawn at the beginning of the year in the first few weeks of January. With so many other things going on in the first half of the year, I probably did not give this planting due attention at the key time of late spring. But even so, the plants seem to have found their own way. They seem to have created their own kind of garden without too much outside help or interference. Opium poppies, bronze fennel, snap dragons, salvias and even sunflowers have joined the herbaceous plants I started with, all unexpected and uninvited incomers, but welcome nevertheless.

For me, the stars of this particular planting have been the strawflowers in dozens of different colour variations. They are like little gems glittering in the sunshine, and still continuing to glow brightly enough through the gloom of the overcast days. I have heard they were a very popular choice once, maybe fifty years ago. Everyone had strawflowers in their gardens back then, but they are not seen much in modern gardens, unfortunately. I have been buying their seeds for the last few years from Chilterns, they are the suppliers I have usually bought things from over the years. I am also fond of Plant World Seeds in Newton Abbot.

Chilterns Seeds was set up nearly fifty years ago by Douglas and Bridget Bowden, working from their kitchen at home as they tried to turn their hobby into a viable business by selling all sorts of seeds, mostly unusual ones that were difficult to find elsewhere. These days, the company is still going strong and is run by their daughters, Heather and Sally, who say they only sell the kinds of things that they like; the seeds for the things they would grow in their own gardens. The Chilterns catalogue is full of treasures and when the spring 2020 edition arrived, I was pleased and surprised to see they had put a close-up of a strawflower on the front cover. So, maybe I am not the only one with a keen interest in those old-fashioned flowers after all.

Moving further on with this September ramble to leave that accidental but colourful glade behind, I am going a little further down the Long Walk with the dry gravel crackling quietly under my feet. The peace of the morning is broken by a sudden loud sound coming from above – helicopters. It must be that the Metropolitan Police have taken to the sky again, this time to observe the Extinction Rebellion protest taking place today just over on the other side of the river. Huge crowds have gathered around Parliament Square to try to pressure the MPs to sign the Climate and Ecology Emergency Bill. The demonstrations have been non-violent. People of all ages and backgrounds have joined in, with the science and research data backing their cause and supporting their arguments. Many thousands of plant and animal species have been lost forever over the last seventy years, according to the World Wide Fund for Nature, who describe this as 'clear evidence of the catastrophic damage human activity is doing to the natural world'.

Last September, Extinction Rebellion organised what was referred to as the Autumn Uprising. It is true there was considerable disruption in the centre of London. Travelling to and from work could be a bit difficult – and some of that was annoying. But it was also exhilarating to take part. To be on Lambeth Bridge for a little while each day with hundreds of strangers, to stand there together to block the bridge to vehicles and turn it into what was called a Bridge of Faith, because there were protesters there identifying with various religions and teachings, uniting in a common cause to pressure for action over climate change. Other bridges were closed in this way as well, blocked by people standing together on them, and there were large gatherings for many days in Trafalgar Square.

Within a few weeks of those protests last autumn, the English, Scottish and Welsh Parliaments made an about turn and announced that there was indeed a climate emergency and promised to take urgent measures. But what has climate change and the increasing pressure on wildlife habitat got to do with gardens?

It is worth remembering that there are millions of gardens all across the world, occupying millions of acres of land. If gardened sympathetically, they can provide homes for a huge range of wildlife, while the trees and plants they contain are not only valuable habitat but also help to fix and store carbon. The gardens of Britain occupy more land space than all the nation's conservation areas and nature reserves combined. How we choose to organise and care for those gardens can make a significant difference to the world around us, and it should be possible to effect positive benefits for the natural environment by making changes to the ways we think about and interact with those gardens, however big or small, however old or new.

It is not only about large historic gardens like Lambeth Palace, but all the small back gardens and yards as well. Whole streets of back gardens, whole towns and cities of gardens, not with the same style or the same plantings, but all with a gardening approach that would put nature first.

I will pause and take a few deep breaths of the early autumn air. I can taste it, the season turning. It tastes a little of fallen leaves, the faintest trace of smoke and something else difficult to identify. I am trying not to focus too much on the helicopter blades whirring up in the sky above my head as I move away from the Long Walk and begin to cross to the other side of the garden. The labyrinth in the grass remains in enigmatic silence to my right and I am watching how the light changes as the tall trees stir in the breeze.

Next on this slow stroll I arrive at the Glades. There are different combinations here from week to week, the colours and textures of the herbaceous perennials coming and going, accented by occasional annuals. I think it has been good year all round, much more than I could have hoped for. And it just keeps going. One or two things have not worked out so far, a few failures, and sometimes those planting failures happen when least anticipated. But that is a significant part of it all. There are different ways of failing and the experience gained from that can be as valuable as any garden success.

Studying the free-flowing lines, it is pleasing that the labour involved in making these new flower beds is evident but the presence of the gardener is not so obvious. The work that needs to be done, pulling unwanted plants, cutting back here and there, removing spent flowers and so on, all has been carried out in ways that the human touch is hopefully never too dominant nor too heavy.

Even as the summer begins to cool, the colours in the Glades are still strong. Flowers often seem to bloom at their brightest just before they begin to fade and die. Colour shades in the garden can change for all kinds of reasons – it could be the weather, it could be the season or even just the time of day. This morning, there is quite a lot of red in evidence, mostly coming from the salvia 'Royal Bumble', which has been self-seeding everywhere. Red becomes more intense as the sun begins to set, so I will wait for evening to see the colours deepen as they catch the last light of the day.

Helenium 'Sahin's Early Flowerer' is also quite prominent now, the petals yellow and red but mostly orange. Gazing at orange flowers for too long can cause us to see flashes of blue. It is an odd feeling. Colour is the light reflecting into our eyes and may not necessarily be the definite and fixed thing it appears to be.

Often we talk about the temperature of different pigments. Green and brown are earthy, so they are warm and steady. Blue is cool and may need a contrasting colour like a deep yellow to bring some life. But there is so much that is invisible to us. For example, the ultraviolet that guides the bees to the nectar or the different temperature hotspots on the petals, encouraging pollinators towards the warmer parts of the flower.

There are vibrations in the waves of flower colours as well, so there is also sound. As I stand here in silence before this planting, I am listening for anything interesting or unusual, but the helicopters above are too loud, so I will have to try another day. Lately, the golden hum of rudbeckia have been to the fore, but also a repeated pairing of contrasting notes is present in the raspberry shades of the persicaria and the violet aster. Tomorrow, there is bound to be something else.

A little further on and I make my final stop on this brief tour. I am at the compost heap, a key part of any garden. Here, there are three separate bays built from old railway sleepers, each of them at a different stage of decay.

One is empty, as it was completely cleared out in the spring and the dark black organic material returned to enrich the garden's soil. Gardeners often call that kind of ideal compost 'black gold'. After that bay had been cleared, the next morning I saw that a hole had appeared in the ground and the hole grew a little bigger each day. Supposing it to be an experimental fox burrow, to check if it was in use I made a light covering with some orange and red sticks that had been left over from pleaching the lime earlier in the year. The following morning, I found that those sticks had been carefully pushed aside like a thin curtain. So, some foxes must have set up home there or at least they had been thinking about it, which means I will have to work our new compost heap around the new inhabitants.

I can picture them emerging from their shallow den at dusk, sniffing at the air and looking up to see what kind of a moon will be shining down on them – cold moonlight is so much better than the hot sun. The foxes wonder what they will find across the garden with the help of the silver moonlight. Discarded fast-food wrappers perhaps, chucked over the wall by careless passers-by in the street. Or tin foil of any kind, always fascinating. Or the prize of all prizes, a mislaid gardener's glove. So many hours could be spent terrorising and tearing that glove to pieces, bit by bit, until it is pretty much unrecognisable.

Before all that fun can begin, they turn their attention, for at least a few moments, to the adornment that has appeared over the entrance to their new burrow. What could that be, those orange and red sticks laid there like some kind of a cover? What could have done that? And why? Somehow, a makeshift door of orange and red had been found and put there without explanation, but with colours that complement the fur coat of a fox quite well, colours in shades of wiry russet. Curious.

POTATO EATERS

t is still September and there is an autumn chill in the air. The time has come to do some digging and I am going to take a look at the potatoes before it gets too late. If they are left too long in the ground, they might start to rot, turn soft and mouldy, with the wet weather coming and the earth around them getting colder. If there is a frost this year, that might finish them off once and for all, as they are southern hemisphere plants.

The potatoes I am checking this morning were planted in four shallow trenches in a back area away from the main garden; a small space, hemmed in by buildings and a high wall heavy with ivy. Mostly hidden away, this little garden has become quite overgrown with all kinds of weeds, stinging nettles as tall as me and spiky brambles. When I was a younger gardener, something as unkempt as this would have given me cause for concern. It would have felt wrong somehow and I would have been inclined to feel some serious action was immediately required. But looking at it now, I can see something else in it, something good. That said, it could do with a bit more attention and even I realise that things may have gone just a bit too far because it is quite difficult to even get into this jungle without being snagged by a thorn or stung by a nettle.

The other day, I went on a train trip to Kent. Looking out of the window, I found there was plenty to enjoy in the unplanned plantings and combinations speeding by outside, especially the profusion of wild buddleias in so many different colours; so many variations of blue and purple. Just common butterfly bushes, but beautiful nevertheless, rich with nectar and therefore attractive to many flying insects, including bees and butterflies. The common buddleias are often overlooked by gardeners perhaps because they are so prolific.

Through the train window, I also could not miss the lush, green foliage of the horsetails in broad sweeps, soft and shimmering clumps beside the polished railway tracks. The horsetail is an ancient plant and can grow rapidly, crowding out other plants with ease, which is why it is probably so rarely seen in gardens. The roots can grow as far as 2m down into the soil and are nearly impossible to eradicate. But their history is long, much longer than ours.

They are believed to have been a key part of a herbivorous dinosaur's diet – and we could eat them ourselves if we wanted to, although they must be cooked first and are supposed to taste a bit like asparagus. Caution must be taken as horsetail plants contain toxins.

As the train sped on further down the tracks, by a stand of small trees I saw a young roe deer emerge alone and pause there, gazing up unconcerned and unafraid as this strange object of metal and glass went hurtling by. Quite a few times, I have seen deer wandering around by train lines, foxes and badgers now and again, and sometimes rabbits hopping about. It makes me wonder about the creatures that are no longer seen in this landscape, the wolves, bears and wild boar. Will they ever be allowed to return?

I have never seen a wolf or a bear but have caught sight of a wild boar on one occasion. It happened in Italy while driving slowly after dark down a rough track winding through the hills above Umbertide, near Perugia. Without warning, something big sauntered out from a covering of trees and undergrowth. A wild boar appeared from the shadows like an enchanted creature strolling out from a book of legends to stand in the night before us, a couple of yards away on the loose shale of the narrow road. Most likely a male, given his size, the boar stood staring at the car, its headlights catching the silver in his whiskers, illuminating the glittering gold discs that covered his dark body. With head raised, he showed his sharp tusks, his breath pluming around his head in the cold night air.

Perhaps he was contemplating challenging us, weighing up whether or not to take on this presumptuous metal creature that was trying to cross his path. Everything was very still as the stand-off in dazzling headlights continued. Our car was only a small Fiat Panda, and although it was certainly a tough thing and had been specially adapted for the rugged, mountainous terrain with a reinforced floor, it still felt as though the wild boar could easily overturn us with a casual shrug, should he wish, to send us spinning down the steep, wooded ravine to disaster. Smoke and mist was rising up from the ground around him. I had switched off the engine a while before but for some reason kept the lights on, I don't know why. Gillian was beside me and I could hear her breathing quietly as we watched through the windscreen, our hearts beating fast.

The wild boar glared towards the car for a few moments more, snorting a little, then seemed to lose all of the little interest he might have had in a skirmish. Looking most unimpressed, he stepped away and very slowly moved off the road, disappearing down the rough hillside into the darkness. We didn't say anything at all but waited there in the silence with the car creaking quietly around us. It was something magical, a moment out of time that we would never forget. I know that sightings of these creatures are said to be becoming common in some parts of the world; the wild boar is even claimed to be becoming a pest in some urban areas. But we had never seen anything like it.

The memory is strong, although standing here daydreaming of places far away with a fork idle in my hand in this little garden won't get the work done. It won't get any of those potatoes out of the ground, if there are even any still growing. I don't know yet, but I will have to see what is down there. It could well be the whole crop has failed this year.

Around 100 had been prepared in the winter; 100 seed potatoes chitted and waiting in the dry darkness of the garden shed for spring to come, so that they could be planted once the danger of frosts had gone. The brambles were cut back and some of the nettles removed to make enough space and then the four trenches were dug to a spade's depth, each marked with a low post at either end. The wrinkled seed potatoes were placed in those trenches at intervals of about 1 ft with loose soil then heaped over them. Every year, I think those wrinkled specimens look so shrunken and unwell that there is no chance they will come to anything. But every year, I have been proved wrong and, once safely buried, the shoots start to grow and the pale edible tubers begin to form in the darkness below the surface.

There are a few things that might spoil them. Potato blight can be a serious problem; a disease that has wrecked entire harvests and had terrible consequences for the people relying on those harvests for their staple food. Eelworms and wireworms can also severely damage a crop with little effort. And then there are slugs. On their subterranean travels, they meet the swollen tubers of the potatoes and often just go straight through them without deviating, leaving a single small tunnel that causes the potato to rot from the inside.

As I begin to dig this morning, I am being careful with the prongs of my fork, aware that they can plunge blindly through the flesh of the buried potatoes and end up ruining them. As there are only four rows here, it will not take long for me to carefully loosen the soil with the fork to both sides of each trench. Then, on my knees, I can work the tubers free with my hands. And as I get down to it, I find there are hundreds of them down there, pale and perfect smooth-skinned ovals like strange eggs of all different sizes, cool to the touch. If kept in a place that is dark and dry, and where mice cannot get at them, these fresh potatoes could be stored for as long as a year.

As no chemicals are ever used, no pesticides or artificial feeds, no copper slug pellets, I have to consider carefully when choosing which varieties of potato to grow. I have to select those that are more resistant to the usual problems of blight or slugs. There are more than 5,000 potato types and over the years I have done some small trials in different gardens with a few of those. A favourite so far has been Rooster, which has an excellent flavour and is firm, with a red skin. Other good ones I have tried are Charlotte and Cara, although they are quite similar to each other. These three seem to be unpopular with slugs and never have any significant problems, in my experience. They are also widely available.

Like the tomato and aubergine, the potato is a valuable foodstuff from the nightshade family. This group also includes some plants such as mandrake or deadly nightshade itself, which have powerful poisonous properties. All the green parts of the potato are toxic but the parts found below ground should be fine to eat; they are rich in protein, vitamins and minerals, as well as carbohydrate and fibre.

Given all that good nutrition, it took a surprisingly long time for them to catch on outside their place of origin in the Andes mountains. It was Spanish soldiers who first brought this new food back to Europe as a minor acquisition from the brutal conquests of South America in the 1500s. The potato was something modest and of novelty interest, perhaps, when compared to the gold and many other precious items they plundered in those times.

Perhaps the Spanish conquistadores had watched from a distance with suspicion as the indigenous people dug those odd, brown objects from the ground; perhaps the soldiers observed how they were kept for months safe in darkened store areas for later consumption. Maybe those soldiers heard the natives' incantations and prayers, even if they had no way of knowing what the words could mean. Here is a translation of a fragment of one Inca prayer:

Oh Creator!
You who gave life to all things,
Multiply also the fruits of the earth,
The potato and other foods you made,
That we may not suffer from hunger and misery.

The Spanish brought the new vegetable back across the Atlantic and farmers in the Canary Islands began to plant their fields with this unusual food. They tried to export them to other parts of Europe but met with little success, even though this was an age when widespread hunger was a common menace, especially for the more rural areas. In England alone, there were seventeen separate famines in the 100 years from 1520. Eventually, the reputation of the humble potato grew and kept growing until it became an essential staple food for most of the world, even if it took several centuries to get there.

Nearly all of the many types we know today have some genetic connection with the potatoes of the Andes, where they have been cultivated for more than 8,000 years. Somehow, those first potato eaters from so long ago must have realised there was something worthwhile in those unimpressive things growing in the rough dirt. After all, as already noted, the leaves and fruits are poisonous – they contain solanine and tomatine, which are harmful to humans. The tubers of those older original varieties had much higher levels of toxins than the potatoes we are familiar with these days and some of those early foragers must have found this out to their cost. Surely it would have been better to stay well away, to search and gather elsewhere for other foods less troublesome?

Possibly those people watched the wild llamas on the mountain slopes, saw them eating dirt and clay before grazing on the poisonous plants. Those clay particles line the animals' stomachs and absorb the poisonous substances, allowing them to pass through the body without causing harm. Perhaps the people took heed of what they witnessed, for they soon began to use a thin soup of soil and water as a dip for their potatoes, imitating in that way the habits of the llamas. I have heard that, even today, you can still buy edible earth soups in some marketplaces in Peru and Bolivia to add to your potatoes, just in case. I would love to see that and maybe sample that edible earth mixture in some busy market square, to talk to the people there and to listen to the tales they might have to tell.

The Andes are the longest mountain range on earth. Should I manage to get there, I would like to imagine slowly clambering up a mountainside, one bright morning, higher and higher, the blue sky getting harder and harder above me as I move further up, the air getting thinner, almost too thin and making me dizzy. Miles above, an immense bird glides in the sunshine, a condor, with its vast wingspan. Inching along a narrow ledge, a few pebbles stutter and slide at my feet to spin down into the deep chasm below.

Tectonic plates shifting beneath these mountains have caused countless earthquakes over many centuries. Life is made even harder by the sudden fluctuations in temperature, the regular landslides and the explosions of molten fire from volcanoes. There are more than 100 live volcanoes in the Andes. Despite these seemingly impossible conditions, somehow the noble potato continues to thrive in its place of origin. It can still be found wild on those rugged and desolate mountain slopes, continuing to grow secretly and silently in the darkness under the stony ground.

The garden is moving into October, and over the last couple of days I have been cutting back some of the herbs in the Chapel Garden with the help of the volunteer team. The idea of this late autumn cut is to keep the plants compact and healthy, preparing them for next spring when they should start to grow quickly again.

Where we are working is alongside the main building, close enough to hear the bell ringing for prayers early in the morning and again in the middle of the day. Looking up from the herbs, I can see the bell tower, one of two medieval towers looming over me, tall structures from the 1400s. Between them is the chapel itself, running from west to east, with high, arched windows of stained glass. It is even older than the towers, dating back to 1234.

As I continue to cut back the fragrant oregano and calamint, I am remembering doing this same thing last year around the same time. When the work was done and the herbs had been shaped into small mounds on the sandy gravel-covered ground, I probably took a few moments to rest on one of the Chapel Garden's six stone benches, my work clothes and gloves sweet with the spicy scent of the many aromatic plants around me – mint, rosemary and thyme.

There is plenty of sage here as well. In olden times, there were some who claimed that by consuming a sage leaf every day in the month of May it was possible to live for much longer than might be expected, even suggesting that eating this herb could somehow unlock the secret of eternal life. That might all seem fairly unlikely but I have heard that chewing a sage leaf every day is supposed to be good for the memory, although the same is said to be true of rosemary.

Looking across the herb garden, I see some green clumps of St John's Wort. In June and July, they were covered with bright yellow flowers like little stars, but they are all over, now the summer has gone. Those plants were grown from seed in the spring and are getting themselves everywhere, among the other herbs and even into the cracks in the paving. Recommended in various parts of the world as a medicinal aid for at least the last 2,000 years, sales of St John's Wort preparations in our times are worth billions as an industry. Some research shows it has value in helping with mental health issues such as depression, but there is other research that describes the herb as interesting but with no clear evidence it does anything that can actually be measured. These conversations and arguments around herbal remedies have often been fairly heated and I suppose they will remain that way for as long as people are mixing herbs into concoctions.

In a few places, some small, bright white daisy flowers are showing. These belong to feverfew; not planted here but another that has seeded itself among the other plants. It is used as a treatment to relieve headaches and migraine, although feverfew is another case where the many controlled tests and studies carried out over the years have not been able to provide any convincing proof of its efficacy. Nevertheless, many people feel they have been helped by the herb and it is widely available to buy as a tea or tincture, so maybe there is something to it after all, maybe the definitive evidence just has not been found yet.

A warm breeze ripples the air and I can smell the sage all around me again, with big swathes of its grey green leaves right behind the stone bench where I'm sitting. Sage has been praised for its beneficial qualities since ancient times, prescribed as a cure for stomach pains and as a balm for skin complaints. Across the Roman Empire, sage was believed to help with memory loss and to improve the brain's functions. The Romans referred to it as 'the holy herb'.

Coming closer to our time, in 2016, the National Centre for Bio-technical Information in North America published the details and conclusions of many years' investigation into sage's potential for treatment of various health conditions, particularly dementia and Alzheimer's disease. While noting more study needs to be done, the lengthy report states, 'The cognitive-enhancing and protective effects of sage are promising'. The research continues, but it seems impossible to deny that the ancients were on to something. It seems their faith in the 'holy herb' was grounded in reason.

While sitting here thinking about the various properties of these herbs, whether they are useful as remedies or not, I have been gazing down into the small circular pond placed at the centre of this garden. Clean water is more valuable than any of these medicinal plants around us – good for the skin and hair, good for digestion and vital organs – an essential for human health. Today, nearly 2 billion people around the world do not have access to safe water – one in four of the human population. How difficult would it be to solve that problem?

The round pond before me does not stir; its surface just reflects back. Something else moves just a little and there is another faint perfume in the air, more spice, a dash of lavender perhaps. We must not cut those lavender bushes too hard, to cut into the mature wood can be quite harmful and could even kill the plant.

Now the fresh clean smell of their leaves mingles with everything else, making me think of freshly washed cotton sheets arranged to dry on bushes by a stream in the sunshine. Like rosemary, the aromatic qualities of lavender can prompt the brain to release serotonin, a natural chemical sometimes called the happy hormone as it relays messages between nerve cells that can help your moods to be more stable, calming anxiety, improving sleep patterns and digestion. Sunshine and exercise can also benefit serotonin levels, which means gardening here on this bright afternoon surrounded by aromatic herbs should be doing all of us some good.

These could be the last few fading days of warmth, with the sun very low in the sky, its golden rays falling softly on the garden. Just the other side of the wall, a red London bus trundles by and, up above, an aeroplane moves in slow motion across the sky, so slow that it seems to be almost stuck to a cloud with stiff wings, leaving a vapour trail behind like an afterthought. There is no movement in the air whatsoever, but even so, a ripple stirs the round surface of the pond.

All the world outside seems faraway and vague, tired as I am from the day's work, just pausing here for a few moments in the last drowsy hour before going home for the evening. I watch Cheyenne walk by with her wheelbarrow. She has been here today helping with the herbs and it has been good to see her in the garden again after a short absence.

Like all of the gardeners, she is a link in the long chain of people that have cared for this place over the last 1,000 years. In a garden with such a long history it can be difficult to make connections to the past when almost everything from the first ten centuries has either gone or been buried below the ground. But the plants themselves can provide their own kind of link. If some of the gardeners from the garden's past were able to travel through time to join us now, no doubt they would be amazed and bewildered by all the changes around them. I imagine the noise would be especially confusing; the cacophony of heavy traffic and those flying things up in the sky, those aeroplanes and helicopters, all so terrifyingly loud. But if they looked down at the herbs growing at their feet in the Chapel Garden, those time-travelling gardeners might find something more reassuring. Maybe they would see the fennel, thyme or lemon balm, herbs that would have been present here through the centuries from the beginning. Those familiar herbs might be like old friends to them.

Another moment of stillness comes and as I glance again into the small pond and look down into the circle of water, I can see figures in the reflected garden behind my shoulder, the faint outlines of the gardeners that were here before through the different ages of this garden. I look away for a moment and then back to the pond but those shapes are all gone, the water just shows the dark reflection of the empty sky.

Perhaps some of those gardeners might have recognised the hyssop here and there, another plant that we grew from seed recently and which returned to the garden last year. Its spikes of deep blue flowers are proving popular with the bees and other insects right now, even so late in the season. Hyssop is a component in the preparation of holy water and so a useful thing to be found growing on a sacred site. I have been trying to restore some of these herbs to the garden, plants that would have been found here centuries ago. There are still some things we do not have, such as saffron or ginger, and going forward it would be good to see if I can reintroduce them as well.

Because of the many tall buildings that have sprung up around us, the present location of this herb garden close to the chapel is probably the only place where herbs could be cultivated successfully in the garden. They need an open flat space with free-draining soil, ideally with plenty of sunshine and the protection of walls or hedges.

I have heard various rumours and proposals put forward by building contractors from outside the palace, who would like to see several extreme changes here. They would like to flatten this whole area of the garden and replace it with a fat slab of hard standing to make a concrete parking area for heavy lorries and trucks. The old yew hedges would be pulled out, the beautiful myrtle trees destroyed and the tall columns of sweet bay trees got rid of as well. The fig trees and roses carefully trained against the wall would also have to go in the general mayhem.

I wonder what our former neighbour, William Blake would have to say. In August 1799, he wrote an indignant letter to the Reverend John Trusler, a prospective client and author of the intriguingly titled book *How to Be Rich and Respectable*. Among many other things, in answer to some of Trusler's criticisms of the poet's ideas, Blake wrote, 'The tree which moves some to tears of joy is in the eyes of others only a green thing that stands in the way', declaring his strong belief in nature as the source of imagination itself.

While considering those thoughts, I am looking at the rich, aromatic carpet of herbs surrounding me. All that would be destroyed by the proposed building project, leaving no more than memories as, for the first time in 1,000 years, this historic site would be left without a herb garden. All to be replaced with nothing but a thick covering of steamrollered concrete. Ah well, we will have to leave them to their steamroller dreams. I am sure their schemes will come to nothing, and in any case, the golden evening is much too good to waste.

The sun is disappearing behind the medieval tower and I have rested quite a while here on this bench. There is no flag flying on those turrets this evening and it is getting cold; the light will be gone before too long. A little bird – a wren, it looks like – is picking up a few stray seeds from the paving as shadows slink across the darkening green of the lawn beyond. The moon is already rising. If the rays touch my face, maybe they will feel as cold as those of the sun are warm. And if we are still here when the stars come out, at least those few visible stars that are not obscured by the glare of the streetlights, it would be good to see if I can remember any of their names.

The names of the herbs around me are easier to remember as I have been working with them for so long. The dictionary definition describes a herb as a plant that is useful, usually with aromatic or savoury qualities, and meant for the kitchen or to make medicines. Some also have spiritual connections, while others are needed when preparing magic spells and potions. Many of the gardeners who have worked in the garden through the ages would have known that the green fennel I was looking at a little earlier has magic properties. Sprigs hung about the doorways are meant to prevent witches coming into the home and placing fennel seeds in keyholes should also keep demons away. All of this is helpful to know.

Among the kitchen herbs growing here are rosemary, sage and thyme. I could add a little flat-leaved parsley to the mixture, and perhaps some lemon sorrel or sweet rocket. There are so many things here in the Chapel Garden, but it is too late and getting too dark to see very much. Herbs for the cooks in the kitchen, herbs for the magician to divine a fortune, herbs for the physician to make the sick well – germander, sweet briar and columbine.

Lambeth Palace had an infirmary for many centuries and, as part of their job, the infirmarers would have been required to find and prepare all kinds of cures and remedies, sourcing the essential materials needed from the plants growing in the garden. We still have quite a few of those ingredients, but I have not mentioned the foxglove nor the opium poppy. Both were strongly in evidence here a little while ago, in vivid colours through the first few months of the summer. Opium is derived from various parts of poppies and is vital for the preparation of morphine and other related drugs. Over 50 per cent of the opium intended for medicinal use is sourced from plants grown in a remote part of Tasmania.

I can picture all those miles and miles of flowers in red and pink, swaying behind high wire fences on the other side of the world, watched over by guards, who may be yawning just a little and brushing away weary tears from their eyes as they monitor the many millions of opium poppies in their care.

NOVEMBER IN COLOUR

After a few false starts, true autumn is here and each day the leaves are falling much faster from the trees. Before settling down to work, I should go for a general wander around the garden again and have a look at what is going on, see what has been happening before returning to the shed to get things ready.

Moving along from the blue gate at the entrance, I notice that something odd is happening in the first of the clipped yew pyramids. Some peculiar grey fur is sticking out from the dark green topiary, almost transparent in the light – a ghostly looking tail that must belong to a grey squirrel. They have found the small red berries of the yew are to their taste and have gone inside the topiary pyramid where they can get at them more easily. The flesh of those small fruits is sweet and safe enough but the seeds within are not, they are poisonous. Every other part of yew is also poisonous, eating even a small quantity of the bark or leaves can be fatal for many animals, including humans. Those grey squirrels seem to know what they are doing. It must be instinct or maybe something else that tells them to avoid those poisonous seeds and leaves and only go for the sweet, red flesh of the berries.

Generally, the squirrels seem to have been in the best of health this year, running free around the garden, although as the temperature falls, they have been even more visible and more active, even a little manic. To prepare for winter, they have even been scavenging from the new olive trees, and this week I have seen dozens of the little grey creatures racing across the lawn with olive branches in their mouths, hurrying to find somewhere to bury their stolen goods, the unripe hard, green fruits. Peppermint oil on the tree trunks might discourage them. I could try that, there is some peppermint in the herb garden.

I suppose there is no choice but to leave them to it for now. The weather has turned for the year and the olives would need a bit more dry heat at this time if they were to properly ripen as far north in the world as London.

Although they may be amusing to see scurrying about on these chilly autumn days, those grey squirrels present some genuine problems. They have a frustrating habit of digging up newly planted bulbs, tulips in particular, for reasons only they know. Often, they take a single bite from the bulb and then discard it on the ground, ruined. Or they plant it somewhere else, completely at random. But it gets much worse than that. Grey squirrels can seriously damage trees and prevent woodland from thriving or even establishing. They take little bites from tree bark often just below a branch junction where the collecting sugars are usually most concentrated, and those bite wounds can lead to the bark splitting as the trunk naturally expands with age. That allows infections to gain access into the tree as the heartwood is exposed, with the protective outer layer damaged – all beginning with those tiny incisions the squirrel has made with its sharp teeth. I have seen a whole avenue of mature beech trees badly harmed in this way.

Looking around as I walk further down the path, I am wondering if there are perhaps too many trees in this garden, shading the light. Or maybe there are not enough. I am wondering if they are too close together or are too far apart. Then I try to imagine the whole garden planted more as a small woodland, with clearings here and there where colourful flower glades could be allowed to grow. That would be quite something to find in the centre of London.

As I pause to consider my idea of more trees, I can hear there are yet more squirrels above me, racing around on the branches as if they were a network of private pathways. Inevitably, they are all grey ones and possibly are all descendants of the ninety-one squirrels released between 1905 and 1907 in Regent's Park, which is only a mile or two from where I am standing now. In most parts of England over the last 100 years or so, these imported greys have forced the smaller native reds out of their habitats to more remote areas of the country where, even in seclusion, their numbers have continued to decline. The greys are more efficient at foraging and therefore leave little for their smaller relatives, while also carrying and transmitting a virus that they can live with but the reds cannot.

Controlling the numbers of grey squirrels is difficult. Shooting, trapping and poisoning have all proven to be ineffective. They are an introduced species and unfortunately that has meant they have no natural predators in England. Goshawks might be one but they would probably not be found in London, although they have been observed in some built-up areas of Europe perched on street lamps as they hunt for pigeons.

Pine martens are another potential predator and have been encouraged in some parts of Ireland, where they have shown themselves to be an efficient natural method to lessen the numbers of grey squirrels. After having been hunted almost to extinction in England, at last some moves have been made to successfully return pine martens to some areas, notably the Forest of Dean, a few years ago. As for an urban sprawl like the one that surrounds me here, I don't know, but I can't imagine pine martens living here. So, the grey squirrels continue to breathe easy for the time being.

My only sighting of a red squirrel occurred in Glasgow. I was sitting on a bench in the park at Kelvingrove looking across at the red brick art gallery opposite when a small, red thing hopped by on the sandy path. I was glad to see it and felt very fortunate. A sunshine-filled Glasgow afternoon and a red squirrel sighting – two unusual things happening in the same day.

While in the city, I paid a visit to the Burrell Collection, intending to see one of the many treasures there, the Wagner garden carpet. This is an impressive object, overwhelming at first sight, measuring more than 5m by 4m. It was created in the early 1600s and shows a fantasy interpretation of a traditional Persian garden with a squarish pond in the middle connected to a series of symmetrical water channels. I had to get up close to see what was going on, there is so much detail, trees and leaves, plants and flowers as well as different birds and many other creatures. There are even fish swimming in the waterways, rippling the water surface as birds take flight around them. Everything is shown in flat perspective and not to scale, but the whole piece is full of magical colour and feeling. Although very few now survive in such good condition, there were many of these garden carpets created in seventeenth-century Persia, perhaps to allow some of the pleasures of the outdoor world to be experienced, even in the depths of winter, by bringing an imaginary version of the garden inside.

Back at Lambeth Palace on this autumn walk, I turn away from the clipped yew pyramids and the avenue of olive trees to make my way towards the tall tulip tree on the lawn, magnificent now, with its leaves in all shades of toffee brown and burnt gold. I will stand beneath the canopy for a few moments and appreciate the November sunlight streaming softly down.

The lawn here under the tree has struggled a bit over the last few years but it is looking a little fuller now. I have been sowing handfuls of grass seed at regular intervals, mostly in the spring but some now, with the ground quite damp and not yet frosted. I think the birds ate a good deal of that seed – pigeons, mostly. They fly down in groups and settle on the grass, standing in lines as if they had been lucky enough to find a free snack bar remaining open at all hours. However, despite the best efforts of those pigeons, some of the grass seed has managed to germinate and the lawn is not as scrappy as it was.

Moving on, I come to the Long Walk where the plane trees are arching high overhead. They are still fairly green, their leaves only just beginning to fade to a pale brown. Off in the distance there are stronger colours, especially those of the liquidambar trees, which are turning to combinations of scarlet, crimson and deep yellow. It may not be the most spectacular autumn blaze ever seen and it may not be the breath-taking colours that can be experienced in parts of North America at the time of leaf fall along the east coast, but it is still good enough to warm the spirits on a cold morning as winter approaches.

As day length shortens, leaves appear to change colour because the green chlorophyll retreats to reveal other pigments, mostly yellows and oranges. Those brighter colours were there all along, protecting the leaves when the sunlight was at its strongest. They were not visible to human eyes, the colours hidden from us by the green pigment. Many different shades of red are becoming apparent at this time, appearing when natural chemicals called anthocyanins are produced from the sugars already present. Why that happens remains uncertain, but it could be another protective measure. To see all these colours at their most vivid, we need cold nights followed by warmer days that are dry and crisp, and that is not the sort of weather for a typical autumn in London, where the nights are generally mild and the days are usually more of a soggy grey.

Shedding leaves has quite a few advantages for the tree because it means that less moisture is lost due to evaporation through the thousands of minute pores on the leaf surfaces. The moisture can then be stored along with amino acids in the trunk, all of which will be useful in the spring when the tree breaks dormancy. No foliage also means that it can be easier to cope with the high winds and storms the winter usually brings because the branches offer less resistance. Most storm damage tends to be caused when trees still have their leaves as each one acts like a tiny sail, and added together this can put quite a strain on the whole structure.

Thinking about it, there is another thing going on with this annual process of leaf fall. By dropping all those dying leaves and covering its own root zone with a yearly mulch of decaying organic matter, the tree is blocking light from reaching any plants lower down that might try to grow at the base, thus removing competition for water and nutrients while making potential space for its own seedlings. Mulching, removing weeds, caring for the soil – it sounds like the sort of things that gardeners are always doing ...

Almost forgotten at this time of year are the common oaks. Their leaves are a dull brown and usually cling on much longer than the leaves of other trees, often still hanging around well into winter. Oaks are one of my favourite trees and I have planted more of them than any other kind. We have only seven at Lambeth Palace. It would be nice to have a few more and maybe I can sneak in another one or two before my time is up here.

The oak trees we do have are full of acorns just now; a popular food for those squirrels, still scuttling about everywhere around me today. Maybe they might bury a few of the acorns they have gathered, they might store them in the ground for later on, only to forget where they are and possibly those helpfully mislaid acorns buried in useful places could germinate and grow to be mighty oaks someday. It could happen.

Oaks are good trees for wildlife. They support more communities of wild creatures than any other native tree, providing habitat and food for bugs, bats and birds, as well as for small mammals such as deer and badgers. They can live more than 1,000 years, although a usual lifespan is more like 200. When mature, oak trees can even shorten their branches as a way of extending their lives when space is pressured, which is quite an amazing thing to be able to do.

It is time for me to hurry back to the shed for the tools or I won't get any work done at all today. But just before that, let me stop for a moment or two by the greenhouse and stand beneath the big ornamental cherry tree. It is almost all soft reds now, very nearly an example of what the experts call 'full tinting', where every leaf is showing colour, something not seen all that often because usually there are always a few loiterers up there that insist on staying green and end up falling to the ground that way.

I hear a sound that is suspicious up high, the sound of yet another squirrel as it descends from the treetop, fixing me with dark, shining eyes while showing off the extraordinary trick of back feet reversal, rotating the ankles 180 degrees to get a better grip while coming down the trunk to ground level. Perhaps this one is going to join some of the others up in the branches of the nearby black walnut tree, which stands tall and stately at the edge of the high mound in the middle of the garden. There may not be any walnuts left on the branches, those squirrels have taken so many unripe ones already and have left the ground below the tree thickly strewn with piles of empty green nutshells.

Or maybe, as a gang, the squirrels are planning a broad daylight return to raid the rows of olives to see if there is anything left for them to steal. Earlier today, I saw one carefully bury a small, green olive fruit in the main lawn in front of the palace, patting everything down neatly with its front paws. As a final touch, the squirrel marked the spot with a butter yellow leaf, which had fallen from a mulberry tree close by. Maybe that mulberry leaf will stay exactly where it was placed, through the winter months, marking the spot, unmoved by the winds, rain and morning frosts.

RAINY DAYS

November has come and most of the flowers are finished for the year. The garden looks a little weary now, just waiting for the autumn to end as the days turn to winter.

Some things keep going, despite the cold and the shorter daylight hours. The salvias began to show their colours in the summer and they are still showing something now, determined not to give up, at least until the first frosts. The velvet purple salvia 'Amistad' has been especially good but the garden has quite a few others. There are so many different ones to choose from, more than 1,000 different species with thousands more varieties and cultivars coming from those species.

Despite the chill in the air, a few insects are still on the wing. I have seen several honey bees venturing out to forage, flying a little more clumsily than usual as they drift from flower to flower with their options diminishing each day. I even saw a bumble earlier today, visiting the deep scarlet 'Royal Bumble' salvia. Bees are not able to see shades of red, they are colour blind to that part of the spectrum, so if it is not the colour, I wonder what attracts them to those red flowers so late in the year? I wonder what they are seeing.

Something else has been going on, not with the 'Royal Bumble' but with the other salvia I was looking at, the purple 'Amistad'. Tiny holes have been appearing at the base of the flower where the nectary swells, perforations made by honey bees who have found a short cut to get at the sweet nectar, bypassing their ancient role as pollinators to try drilling little holes and extracting it in that way. If no pollination takes place, the flowers will not set seed and in the long run, everyone loses out, including the bees themselves. While this is an interesting development, hopefully this adaptation is not going to become general among pollinating insects.

Meanwhile, as I have been observing the salvia flowers, the sky above me has darkened and a light rain is beginning to fall. This brings some of the last leaves spinning down from the trees onto the paths, paving and already sodden grass. A faint wind gets up from the south-west and more leaves come down to the ground. Light levels are too low for effective photosynthesis to make energy so it is more efficient if the tree can shed the leaves at this time of the year. A very thin, hard layer like a callous has formed where each leaf stalk joins a twig or a branch, described as an abscission layer, a row of tiny cells creating a seal so that the leaf can be dropped without leaving an opening that could potentially allow an infection into the trees. Every autumn, this natural miracle is going on all around us with every single one of those leaves, billions of them responding to the changing season.

As the afternoon gets darker, more leaves fall. With the help of the volunteer team and the other gardeners, I will rake up what I can and put it into big empty bags. We have a tatty collection of old ton bags, which once held sundry materials like sand or gravel, and we now reuse them for leaf-collection purposes. At times, it feels too much, as though the waves of leaves will never end, but we continue with the raking and collecting and by the end of the year, the last leaf will have been picked up. Some of them can be added to the compost heap – the oak and hornbeam, sycamore and beech. They will usually break down to dark organic matter in less than a year. The fig leaves are even quicker, they only need maybe a week or two to decompose.

Other types can take much longer, especially the evergreens, such as holly or bay. Longest of all seem to be the plane tree leaves. The waxy cuticle that covers each one is almost impermeable and often piles of them can be found in corners of the garden that look to have been lying around for years without ever changing or even beginning to rot down. I have asked quite a few other gardeners about their experience with plane leaves and the general opinion seems to be it takes about ten years for them to decompose. That is a long time, particularly given that it is reckoned more than half the street trees in London are plane trees. One of the big questions is where do all those plane leaves go, where can they be stored while they gradually break down so slowly into mulch?

There is a long hornbeam hedge at the north perimeter of the garden and all our plane leaves are put out of the way behind there, along with any of the other slow ones. Every four or five years, the lower levels of this pile can be dug out and there should be some good dark organic material further down – good leaf mould to make a mulch for the soil. Eventually everything returns into the earth, including the leaves, maybe even the plane leaves, and the cycle of regeneration keeps going.

The gardeners are not the only creatures removing fallen leaves from the paths, lawns and flower beds. There is a huge population of earthworms living with us and each night they come out after dark to pull some of the dead leaves down into their burrows, chewing on them and softening them to digest them more easily. Looking at all the worm casts everywhere, I can see those slim subterraneans have been very active these last few weeks. The recent downpours are the cause and the rain has brought them up from their burrows. For many years, it was said that the fear of drowning in waterlogged ground could be the reason why they make their way towards the open air when it rains. Research has shown that is probably not the case, more that when things are slippery and wet and you're a worm, it is much easier to move around by sliding along, to search out new habitats and food sources, even to look for a mate. Although they are hermaphrodite, they still need another worm to be able to reproduce and can visit a prospective partner's burrow as many as twenty times before anything happens.

The rain keeps falling and I am seeing more and more of the tiny black casts of perfect topsoil left by the worms on the lawns as they come up towards the light. There are others who are aware of this response to the wet weather. White and grey gulls are gathering on the grass now and when there is an occasional dry spell, they drum the ground impatiently with their yellow, webbed feet as they perform a peculiar bird dance to imitate the rhythmic thrumming of the rain, tricking any unwary worms up to the green surface of the lawn, where they can be caught by the birds and swallowed whole.

It is said there are around a million worms in an acre of healthy soil. That would be 10 million earthworms in the garden if everything is looked after well. Except for the Arctic, worms can be found in all parts of the world, even under the oceans, and their activities in those places are vital to all kinds of life. They digest decaying organic matter and, by natural chemistry, turn it into a growing earth medium that is rich in nutrients, including essential nitrogen and phosphorus. With their help, in a teaspoon of healthy soil there should be more than a billion living organisms, most of them invisible without a microscope. There are more living organisms in that teaspoon than there are stars in the night sky.

For many of us, gardens are the places where we have our most direct contacts with nature. Maybe that is why gardeners talk so much about the importance of composting and recycling green waste, doing everything possible to keep that top layer of the soil profile healthy and full of life and encouraging those billions of soil organisms to continue with their cycles. The earthworms are a crucial part of nature's cycles, working away quietly in their medium of mud, soil, clay and earth.

I am trying to imagine all the strange things they must encounter down below ground in this garden as they move around, some of the same kinds of things I encounter when digging shallow holes to prepare for planting. Just below the surface, there are patterns of old bones and fragments of broken glass, oyster shells and old rubble, broken bricks mostly, and an array of rusting metal that must have had a use once. But whatever those rusting chunks of metal were used for, it is now hard to figure out what that could have been. Bits of pottery and china often turn up as well, so much that I would think if enough could be salvaged, it might be possible to reconstruct a cup, mug or plate, or perhaps something even grander and more complicated.

There used to be a large pottery just around the corner from here on Lambeth High Street. It was bought up in 1826 by Doulton &

Watts of Vauxhall to develop further their already successful business making stoneware bottles, jugs and jars. The company grew in prestige and eventually became Royal Doulton. It is possible that some of the stoneware and china we keep finding buried in the garden came from them, but it is all in fragments now.

Something else we often find are little pipes for smoking tobacco, made of white clay. There are hundreds of them down there. Nothing completely intact has been found so far. All of them are in pieces after so many hundreds of years buried in the soil. Smoking became a popular practice all over London from the 1600s and the clay pipes we find date back to that time. There are many broken bits and pieces stored in a large box at the back of the shed, varying in style according to the fashions of the time, but all made with a little bowl at one end to accommodate one small plug of tobacco. Maybe the pipes could be catalogued someday. Perhaps they could be displayed in a glass case as a museum exhibit.

Moving beyond the garden walls for a little while, if I were to walk for around 10 miles in a south-easterly direction and leave the old marshes of Lambeth behind, I might eventually arrive in Bromley. I could keep going a little further until Down House and its gardens come into view. This property was once the home and workplace of Charles Darwin and nowadays is managed by English Heritage, who open it to everyone so we can explore the house and garden at our leisure. We can even admire the beautiful blue-painted greenhouse that Darwin instructed to be built so that he could study how some of his less-hardy plants were growing. A small tunnel passageway was included in the structure of the greenhouse to allow pollinating bees to come and go.

If there were enough time, I would like to take a stroll up to the small woodland at the far end of the grounds to visit the Sandwalk, laid out among the trees where Darwin paced several circuits each day to think things through without interruptions, all the while surrounded by nature. The walk is quite hidden away and is reached via the vegetable garden. Once in the woods, through the gaps in the trees the green fields of Kent can be seen, rolling away towards more woodlands in the distance.

At a certain point on the path, it was Darwin's habit to prepare a small group of stones and then gently kick one away each time he had completed a circuit. In that way, he would not be distracted by having to count how many times he had been around the path and could concentrate on his thoughts. As I stand there looking along the pale track, more stone than sand these days, the last leaves of the autumn are falling slowly from the trees as a gentle rain drifts a little and then stops.

Darwin's final manuscript was completed at Down House in 1881, six months before he died. It investigated the subject of earthworms; something he had been pondering for a long time. More than forty years before completing this book, he had presented a paper in 1837 to the Geological Society on the importance of the role of worms in soil formation. In that same year, he wrote in his journal the firm conclusion that 'it is absurd to think of one animal as being higher than another'.

When *The Formation of Vegetable Mould through the Action of Worms* came out, it was an immediate success, surprisingly selling more copies at that time than any of his other works had, including *On the Origin of Species*. Although it was not the aim, his findings also changed gardening forever, as he highlighted and proved the vital significance of those humble underground earthworms in helping all kinds of plants to grow. It had been believed, up to then, that earthworms somehow damaged the soil and could even cause weakness in roots but after Darwin published his last book, there would be no reason for an earthworm to ever be underestimated again. He suggested that it could be asked, 'If there are any other animals which have played such an important part in the history of the world as these lowly organised creatures'.

Perhaps there is still something of Charles Darwin at Down House today, deep in thought in the woods as he shuffles through the golden, crimson leaves, where early winter shadows are quivering, his silver-white beard catching the light as he moves along with his trusty walking stick. Maybe he is considering again the valuable activity of those enquiring beings moving under the ground beneath his feet, those mysterious earthworms.

HAND TOOLS

When a new gardener begins in a new garden, on their first day, no doubt they would want to spend some time in the tool shed looking over the machines and other things that hopefully will be of help to them with the work lying ahead. The bright oranges and reds of the big ride-on mowers parked, waiting quietly, can be quite dazzling at first, and there is the smell of petrol as well. A mixture of petrol, oil and cut grass always hovers around those machines, a little intoxicating. Something aromatic and slightly sweet is always in the air, a blend of garden elements difficult to describe exactly.

Standing in the big shed at Lambeth Palace, I am inspecting some of the equipment stored here. The brush cutter, the hedge shears and the leaf blower are all present and correct. They are of a newer design and are battery powered, just as efficient as the older versions, which ran on petrol, but much quieter and cleaner. Before long, the remaining petrol and diesel lawn mowers will also be replaced and then everything will be electric. Maybe solar panels could be installed on the roof and, in that way, renewable energy could be sourced to run the machines.

On this cold winter morning, I move further into the darkness of the shed, going towards the collection of assorted spades, shovels and forks hanging in a line on hooks, glinting a little as they catch the faint light coming in through the open door. Overhead, there is a sudden sharp sound. Those restless squirrels again. I can hear a couple of them are skating across the roof up above before they slither down the drainpipe, hurrying away to cause trouble elsewhere. And that other scratching noise coming from under the floor, I'm not sure, but I think it could be mice. That would be something for the cat to take care of, wouldn't it?

If this was my first working day at Lambeth Palace running the rule over the tools and equipment, I would quickly realise they are a mixed lot – trowels and knives, wire brushes and yard brooms, loppers, shears and so on. There are a few hammers as well, a couple of them are quite heavy. I can see the rakes leaning neatly against the wooden boards of the shed wall, good rakes that will always be needed. There are assorted secateurs on a shelf among some of the everyday tools essential for garden work. A few other things that are more puzzling are sitting on that dusty shelf, including a roll of grey duct tape next to a box full of screws and some keys of different sizes. Who knows what they might lock and unlock?

There is a range of various saws as well, most of them too far gone and stiffened with age to be of much use. But maybe they could be restored. Maybe they could work again and emerge as something useful from the general collection of discarded tools.

One of the saws looks especially elderly, leaning over in the corner, out of the way, and almost hiding as if a little shy, its blade with rusting metal teeth blunted after so many years with nothing to do and no attention at all. That old saw is a big thing and two people would be needed to operate it, one at each end. Briefly grasping one of the handles, I can feel the contours of the wooden grip, worn and shaped by the many different hands that have worked with it through the years. Maybe a few trees were felled in the grounds right here, using this very blade, chopped down for firewood or else removed because someone decided they were in the way.

Thankfully, all the trees in the garden are protected by law now. There are more than 100 mature specimens at present, every one covered by a preservation order and permission from the local authority has to be requested to work on them. Permission has to be given even to remove a damaged branch of medium size. With all that in mind, it seems unlikely the ancient saw I am holding here will ever have to work again. I will put it back in its corner to continue its long rest.

I am looking to see what else there is on those shelves. Some scissors, twine, a couple of fairly useless offcuts of yellow hose and various bits of iron chain. I don't know what the chain is being kept for; I can't think of any garden use.

There are quite a few tools stored here that are damaged or broken, stacked away behind other things and unlikely to ever be picked up again. Last year, we had a visit from some volunteers for The Tools Shed, an organisation that gathers old garden equipment from various collection points throughout the country to have them sent to prisons. Once there, some of the prisoners refurbish and repair the tools in their workshops, learning new skills and techniques in basic carpentry and metalwork, for which training is given. Possibly these new skills could open a door for the prisoner later on, once their term is complete. They might find new kinds of work opportunities.

The volunteers from The Tools Shed brought in some examples of forks and spades that had been carefully mended and returned to something near their former state. They looked in fine shape. Most of the refurbished tools are given away as donations to schools and various community projects involving green spaces. The old, unwanted things we have in the shed here can be gathered and taken to the nearest collection point, which for us is in Brixton.

I have picked up an old pair of edging shears with their handles worn smooth, made of wood that was once painted red. These shears must have done a lot of work in this garden over the years. They are heavy in my hands now but well balanced and easy enough to hold. Even through my garden gloves the wood feels cold and I shiver a little to think of all the other hands that have held these old shears and the almost imperceptible contact I am making with gardeners who are no longer here.

It is time to take the tools I need and get out to work in the winter garden. There are one or two items I will have to mark absent from the shed, in particular, something that was useful to me many years ago when I was trying to be a junior *jardinero* back in Barcelona. We worked with many of the same hand tools that are normally used in England, although one essential piece of equipment over there is the *azadón*, known as a mattock in English, and not used much by gardeners here. It has a short, wooden handle going down to the metal head that usually has a flat blade on one side with a sharper point on the other, resembling a pickaxe. For digging, hoeing or weeding, I found the *azadón* to be quite a versatile and helpful instrument.

Back in the shed at Lambeth Palace, there is no *azadón* to be found. I am lingering here to put off the moment of going out into the cold, although it is probably colder inside the shed than out in the garden. I will take a last look at what else there is to check over. Not so long ago, we had a good supply of hand forks neatly stacked on the shelf but quite a few of them are missing now. They will be somewhere in the compost heap, I expect, mislaid in buckets of weeds and accidentally buried to then re-emerge next year when the compost is turned. Those precious hand tools will be a little worn out by the experience but hopefully will still be usable and not too rusty. I shiver again to think of it as the temperature drops further in here.

I have the tools I was looking for and will now go out to get some work done. My secateurs are placed in a holster on my hip. I will need them as I am going to do some winter pruning. There are more than 100 shrub roses in the garden, types that will repeat flower through the summer months if the time can be found to keep removing the spent blooms. There are several species types here as well, sweet briar roses and dog roses, rosa glauca and rugosa. The technique for pruning them is different and it is better to leave some of the mature longer growths from the previous year.

It is a mid-December morning but there is no frost on the surface of the lawn as I walk over towards the raised terrace where the roses are growing. By now, most of the green leaves have fallen from them and

I can get a clearer view. The first thing to do is check for the three Ds, that is, anything dead, diseased or dying. With my secateurs sharpened and ready, I carefully remove all those unwanted stems. From time to time, I clean the blades so as not to pass on anything unwanted from plant to plant, problems such as grey mould that may weaken the rose. I have found a small handful of sage leaves or a few sprigs of lavender are good for cleaning my secateurs as I work.

Once the weak growth has been removed, I begin to open up the centre of the plant, trying to create a bowl shape, keeping that bowl shape in mind throughout. Stems that are growing inwards are cut away, as well as those that are crossing each other or rubbing. I am trying to anticipate where other stems might grow inwards, given the chance, and remove them to prevent problems later on. With the centre of the rose bush open like this, there should be good air flow, which can help prevent fungal growth building up while also allowing smaller birds to get in without being spiked by thorns. Those birds will feed on any aphids that might be gathering and so help the rose stay strong and healthy.

The blades need to be sharpened often, so I have a small whetstone with me for that purpose. Rough or frayed cuts from blunt blades will only make difficulties for the plants later on, leading to dieback and infections. Believe it or not, these red secateurs of mine have been with me through thick and thin for more than twenty years: Felco 2, ever faithful, thank you for all the help.

When the *New York Times* surveyed forty-nine different models of garden secateurs in May 2020, they put the Felco 2 at the top of their list. I expect Felix Filsch, the founder of Felco, would have been proud. His brilliant idea was to take a basic garden tool and elevate it to a crafted instrument of the highest quality that would last a lifetime, ensuring that individual parts could be supplied at a low cost to replace those that had worn out. He bought an old watch-making factory in the late 1940s, where he set about designing and making his new secateurs.

You can still find second-hand Felco watches, they are Swiss-made but do not seem to be connected to the company making Felco secateurs, which is quite puzzling. They are expensive. I have seen a few on eBay and most are a quite a bit more than £100, so maybe they are for the collector only. That said, I wouldn't mind looking down while pruning and seeing my old Felco watch on my wrist with my old red Felco secateurs in my hand. Today, the descendants of Felix Filsch are still directly involved in the running of the company and have remained true to their motto, 'Swiss precision made to last'.

Taking a brief rest from the pruning work, I check the tools around me again. I have my trusty secateurs, a hand fork and bucket as well as a rake. But no helpful *azadón* close by in case it were required to do a little extra digging or hoeing. I should get one or two, even if they have to be imported from Spain; they might come in useful. I make another brief pause to consider what other essentials might be needed for this day in the garden. The cat could be required in some capacity but she is nowhere to be seen. Perhaps it is too cold for her and she has remained indoors to carry out her own work around the place, hopefully to include the mice I heard earlier running about under the tool shed.

When she decided to take up residence in the gardeners' quarters, for the first few weeks in her new home she would occasionally bring in a gift to the small office at the back in the form of a dead mouse. She presented them in perfect condition, killed but somehow unmarked, neatly arranged in a crescent shape on the floor below my desk. Early some mornings, while checking things over before heading out to the garden, I would feel an odd lumpy thing under my feet, remembering too late that the little lumpy thing was a dead mouse. It was a simple gesture, I suppose, a gesture that said, 'This is what I do, this is my nature'. No hand tools needed, just sharp teeth, claws and a great deal of patience. As she became more confident of her place, the gifts became less frequent, hardly any at all anymore.

THE SPIRIT OF THE BEEHIVE

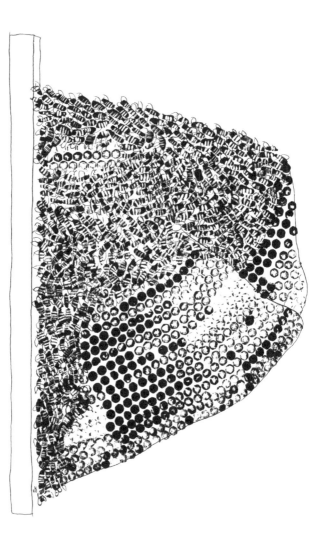

On moving an old piece of wood or turning over a stone in a garden, nearly always I find that there will be something alive underneath. It could be a worm; it might be a millipede or a slug; it could be a toad, a beetle or something else altogether. A few days ago, I had to shift some slowly rotting branches from beside the path, and in doing so briefly uncovered a pair of newts that were hiding there. They were lying close together, motionless, curled up neatly with their heads touching as if they were embracing. Quickly, I replaced their wooden cover. They were so peaceful and so still that it occurred to me perhaps they were too still. I thought maybe they had crawled in there to die together, their eyes closed tight as they lay on the old leaves under the rotting branches.

To find out for sure, I returned the next day and looked again. The two of them had gone, so they must have been resting or sleeping after all. They were smooth newts, the colour of soft gold with faint stripes down their bodies, and there are hundreds of them living in the garden, moving around in the undergrowth most of the year then swimming about in the ponds through the summer months. They are nocturnal and spend most of the daytime under stones or fallen branches, sometimes even in the compost heap. From autumn to early spring, they usually hibernate.

Now that it is the middle of winter, I wish I hadn't picked up those crumbling logs and disturbed the two of them sleeping there quietly. But those branches had crept a little across the pathway and it would have been easy to trip up on them for anyone not paying enough attention and my gardener's instinct kicks in at once to oblige me to move the hazard. Slips, trips and falls – these are the most common accidents in a garden.

There is no protection for smooth newts under the law, unlike their close relative the great crested newt, which is now an endangered species. They are bigger and darker, with a pronounced jagged crest running along their backs that makes them look a little like miniature black dragons. A few of them have been sighted here in the past, where the old pond used to be at the far end of the garden. A big building project for a new library has been going on in that area over the last three or four years and in the course of the work, the contractors removing the old pond were lucky enough not to find any great crested newts in their surveys. If they had, it might well have slowed their project down quite a bit. Hopefully, the protected newts found a safe place to hide while the builders were there and from that safe place they might have watched the workers in their fluorescent yellow hardhats, walking from one huge, temporary structure to another. Maybe the little creatures blinked up at the monumental crane above; perhaps they felt the heavy weight of the massive mechanical diggers sliding around on caterpillar tracks as they squashed the soil down to compacted mud.

Great crested newts can live for around fifteen years, so perhaps they were able to wait it out, just waiting until all that construction work came to an end. Or perhaps they just moved on to somewhere else a little less overcrowded. To make space for the new library, some trees had to be removed and a new site had to be found for the garden's essential heaps of compost and leaf mould. The beehives also had to be relocated.

Now the building is finished, I am standing in the garden looking up at it and the thousands upon thousands of orange bricks. To protect the valuable books and fragile manuscripts from damaging natural light, there are no windows in those outer walls, at least as far as I can see. That is not quite true, there are three small ones towards the top. As I look up, I can see someone working from a high rope fastened to a support on the roof, suspended there to reach the surfaces of those three windows to clean them.

There is a viewing area at the top a kind of elevated terrace with much glass and dark grey cladding. But our neighbours at St Thomas' Hospital have a project of their own that might obscure the new views from that rooftop terrace. They plan to build some even taller structures to include a vast triangle of glass and steel flanked by high-rise towers, giving them more space for their work and as a means to provide vital funds for the hospital itself. These proposed constructions could overshadow the new library building in the garden as that short stretch of Lambeth Palace Road continues to change in character.

Standing on the garden path while trying to picture the new skyline that will soon appear, I am thinking back to the day, five years ago, when I helped Dale the beekeeper move all the hives from this area. How green and tranquil it all was back then. With a trailer, we took the beehives to a new site beside the west wall, which I hoped would look like a small village for honey bees, placing each of the colonies in their separate hive or houses, lifted off the ground on short stilts. Some paving slabs had been found by chance behind the tool shed and these were laid on the ground equal distances apart, all carefully measured, and the slabs levelled to be as flat as possible. Then Dale and I placed each of the twelve hives on its own square stone. Now it does look a bit like a small village on stilts, or at least it does to me.

Honey bees are social creatures and everything they do is for the greater good. If necessary, they will even give up their lives to protect the others in their group; that is the true spirit of the beehive. Maybe the change of location has had some benefits for them as the tree canopy above is higher and thinner than in their old place. That could be an improvement for them. Generally, they prefer to fly upwards when they leave the hive, they do not like to exit on a horizontal line where they would have to dodge around low branches and other annoying obstacles. They want to go upwards to the sky – straight up and out into the open. Sheltered by the high wall behind them, they can rise freely through the air, wings beating more than 200 times a second, as they set off to find forage, which will mostly be nectar from flowers. They will also need to collect small amounts of water that have gathered here and there. They can often get that from rain puddles.

Sometimes, scouts are sent out first. On returning to the hive, they perform a series of movements in a figure of eight, which has become known as the waggle dance. It is a way of communicating to the others where there is something of value, a dance to tell the bee community how far away and in which direction the potential forage can be found. Usually, the dancing scout will even have samples of nectar and pollen on her body so that the others can judge its quality and decide if the expedition is worthwhile.

The existence of bees on earth goes back far longer than human history. Bee fossils have been found preserved in pale yellow Burmese amber that are 145 million years old. Today, there are around 270 different bee species in England but only one species of honey bee, identified as vital pollinators if many of our ecosystems are to survive in the coming years.

Through the spring, summer and autumn at Lambeth Palace, they go out each day to gather the nectar that will be made into honey back in their hives. They find some flower colours especially attractive; blue and purple are generally preferred, while violet is a particular favourite. Those colours have been emphasised in the Glade plantings near their hives, with asters, verbenas and echinacea, among others, and this seems to have worked out well. Over the last year, more than 400 herbaceous perennials have been added to these areas and this has been good for the bees, and other wild creatures, and also good for any human beings who might happen to be passing by. But on this winter day, pretty much all of it has gone over. It is mostly dead stems and seed heads, with just a few faded blooms still surviving through the December cold. Not much is left.

However, the bees are still alive inside the hives, even though the temperatures have fallen to near zero. Unless it reaches at least 10 degrees above, they probably will not come out to see if there is anything to be had from those few remaining flowers. Winter foraging should not be essential for them and although some of the honey they had prepared has been harvested and taken away by the beekeepers, there should still be enough remaining for the bees. Just in case there is a shortage, the beekeepers also provide a regular supply of sugar syrup as a reserve to get through these cold days.

For thousands of years, humans have been gathering honey. The first records of organised beekeeping date back to the beekeepers of ancient Egypt, where some believed the beautiful honey-making insects to be born from the Sun God's tears.

Inside the hives, the worker bees will be clustered towards the centre to keep the queen warm. In a huddle, they will be make quick shivering movements with their wings and their bodies to try and maintain a reasonable temperature. By now, all the male drone bees will have died off. Their lives are fairly short, usually no more than fifty-five days, their only objective being to mate with a queen when the time is right. Sometimes they can be seen gathered in groups, maybe on a tree branch, just hanging about and waiting for something to happen. They do not do any work, no gathering of nectar or pollen for them, no building or repairing of the hive's honey combs, and should they try to sneak in to overwinter inside, the resident worker bees won't put up with that and will physically force them out to perish in the cold.

Protecting the hive and guarding the welfare of the queen are essential for the worker bees. They need to keep intruders and predators at a distance and have their sting as a last resort to do so. If you go near to the hive, you might find a few bees will give you a gentle butt with their heads as a warning to discourage attention and steer you away. In all the years I have worked close to honey bees, I have only been stung three or four times. On a rainy day last summer, I was doing something in the area close to the hives when a bee flew down inside one of the black wellington boots I was wearing and stung me on the ankle. It was painful and I told Dale the beekeeper about it next time I saw him. He was not especially impressed. He looked down at my boots. 'Were you wearing those?' he asked.

'Well, yes, I was.'

'Then what did you expect to happen?'

It was a fair point, I thought to myself, a very fair point.

The harvest of honey that Dale has been able to take from the hives has more than doubled in the last two years, so I think we must be doing something right, providing plenty of diverse potential forage for them throughout the year and developing the planting range as much as possible while ensuring a good framework of native plants is maintained.

The general trend in England has shown declining honey yields. Over the last twelve months, each hive in London has produced an average 10.4kg of honey, a significant drop from the 18.8kg of the previous year. Our hives have not followed that pattern at all, they have gone from 21.7kg in 2019 to 23.5kg, on average, in 2020. As London bees, they have produced more than double what might have been expected.

Dale's high standards of beekeeping have played a key part in this and there may also be other factors to consider. The Beekeepers Association surveyed their members and they identified the availability of a wide variety of abundant flowers to forage as the most significant reason for the general success of a hive. Weather patterns also have an impact, while gardeners not using any chemicals or poisons in the garden work seems to have been significant as well.

Walking away from the apiary and looking across at the plants in the Glades, I can see they are mostly different shades of brown and grey now, with not much alive, but I notice there are a couple of catananche flowers still showing violet blue. They were something new that I added last spring and they threaded through the beds all summer. It is an open flower and therefore easy for a flying insect to access, the petals arranged as a guide, directing the pollinator to the centre of the bloom where the nectar is found, the ultimate prize. If you look closely enough, the delicate black stamens even resemble bees legs dipped in gold.

Before leaving the bee hives and returning to work, one last thought. In Shakespeare's play *Henry V*, the Archbishop of Canterbury gives some useful advice to the royal court, emphasising the value of community and cooperation:

> ... for so work the honey bees,
> Creatures that by a rule in nature teach
> The act of order to a peopled kingdom.

GOING TO TRAFALGAR SQUARE

There was thin layer of frost on the ground, early on this January morning. These first weeks of the year can be hard going for gardeners, although over the years I have found that February can be even a little worse, bringing the coldest days of all, when the wind turns and tends to come from the east to bring the icy air over from Siberia, more piercing and sharp enough to find any slight gap there might be in my various protective layers of winter work clothes.

The heavy clouds are a strange yellowish purple and a few flakes of snow are beginning to drift down. It is below zero but the snow will not settle, melting as soon as it touches the ground. To cope with these chilly days, finding suitable gardening gloves can be difficult. Something is needed to keep my hands warm while also being thin enough so I can feel what I am doing. They have to be close fitting around the fingers.

I went for double gloves this winter: first a thermal pair, then knitted fingerless ones worn over the top of those. I have heard that in the old days gardeners used to have devices to help them, such as slowly smouldering sticks of charcoal enclosed in small bags made of canvas or velvet to keep in their pockets – something to help them warm their fingers now and then. I don't know about that, maybe I would be wondering the whole time if my pocket was about to catch fire and that could be quite offputting while trying to do some of the winter pruning and pleaching. It could be quite risky, up on top of the tall ladder with a pocket full of fire.

The oldest gloves in existence are said to those that were found in King Tutankhamun's tomb. They were made over 3,000 years ago, crafted from very fine linen and would not be of much use for outdoor work. Those gloves might be more practical for holding the reins while driving the royal chariot through town, perhaps. Tutankhamun had others to garden for him, but would have been well versed in the essential importance of plants in Egyptian history and culture. More than thirty different types of plant material and seeds were found in his tomb, with fig, olive and grape vine all there, as might be expected. Pieces of cornflower, coriander and barley were also present. The black seeds of nigella too, along with many small samples taken from trees, including willow, cedar and oak. Material derived from the acacia tree was also identified with his burial offerings.

Here at Lambeth Palace, the January morning slowly turns to afternoon. I am going to leave work just a little earlier than usual today. I'm going to slip away via the back gate.

There is an exhibition to see – Albrecht Dürer at the National Gallery – and Rose is going to meet me in Trafalgar Square with the tickets. They are timed for a particular slot, which means I must not be late. The walk is just over a mile, so it should take around twenty minutes, but looking at my watch I see that somehow I have got less than half that. There is no time to hang around. I must get a move on and get out of here.

Leaving by the back gate, with its complicated magnetic lock, I go on to the street and turn at the first corner into the small alleyway that leads to the park next door. It is like another world in there with big areas of neatly mown grass. There are hard tennis courts and artificial football pitches and some good trees with a mixture of shrubs to the edges. Underfoot, the ground is hard as if still frozen and there are dark imprints showing the shapes of leaves on the pathways, faint outlines of the autumn leaves that were swept away weeks ago but which have still left their stamp on the tarmac for a while before fading to nothing. I have to hurry over that path, slippery though it may be. There is no time to lose as I shuffle along as quickly as I can, fairly awkward as I keep my cold hands in my pockets.

Set into a stretch of the paving below me there are a series of thirty-two circular plaques commemorating significant points in the history of Lambeth between the years 1000 and 2000 – a Millennium Pathway to highlight some special events and people. Just now, I am stepping on the one that tells me Westminster Bridge was opened in 1750, one of the oldest of the thirty-five bridges that span the Thames in central London and the very bridge I am heading for now. But I should have been there at least five minutes ago.

In the park, there is activity of different kinds on all sides, with movement and sound swirling around me. School children are playing football on one of the evergreen AstroTurf pitches. More small children are gathered on the touchlines, their shouts of joy high and wild as they are out in the open air for a few hours. The sound of a thin whistle trills above it all, made by a referee or teacher, but nobody seems to notice and the game just goes on, as chaotic as before.

There are people on most of the benches around the park, sitting quietly. It is still lunch break for many of them and they have found a retreat in the green space even in winter, leaving behind the workplace, if only for a short while. Around 40 per cent of London is made up of gardens and parks that are open to everyone – more than 35,000 acres across 3,000 sites of varying size. These green spaces are precious to all of us who live in cities, wherever they may be.

The time is moving quickly by and now I know that I am going to be late for the exhibition. There are so many distractions and I have to get on my way and out of this park without any further detours or delays. Two people are sitting on the bench I am passing by, wrapped up against the cold in big coats, wearing heavy gloves with warm, woollen hats for their heads.

'It is what it is,' says the first.

'Yes, we are where we are,' agrees the second, with a frown.

What any of that means I could not say, but I cannot pause to think it over just now. Looking towards the fence on the left, I can see Lambeth Palace on the other side, its pale yellow sandstone catching the winter sunlight. The tops of the trees are visible as well, branches bare now the leaves are all gone from the canopies. The trees are so familiar to me as I see them every day but somehow they seem quite different from here; they look like strangers when viewed from this distance.

There are more sudden high shrieks as another goal hits the back of the net in the school game. Leaving the cheering crowd to their celebrations, I go from a fast walk to a half-run and at last make it to the exit gate that leads into Lambeth Palace Road. There are frosted weeds growing in most of the pavement cracks here and up against the wall. It is quite amazing how they manage to find a way in, to grow in such unpromising places. Perhaps they have been missed by the council's regime of glyphosate spraying, which seems to have been more ruthless than ever over the last year. For me at least, I don't mind at all seeing those weeds growing there.

Back in the garden office, there is a photocopy pinned to the wall of Dürer's masterful watercolour *The Great Piece of Turf*, which he painted in 1503, showing in very close detail several of the same plants I am briefly studying now growing in the pavement, just outside the park. His painting includes the humble dandelion, plantain and yarrow, as well as several different types of grass. It is an extraordinary picture, contrasting the seemingly casual approach to the composition with the precise care taken to render each of those wild plants, going far beyond dry depictions to suggest something deeper regarding the strong character and qualities of these so-called weeds. It feels like a real chunk of turf captured exactly as it was and not idealised or artificially prettified for the sake of aesthetics or theories of proportion. Quite why, in this watercolour, he chose to celebrate and foreground such a modest subject gives much pause for thought. He once stated that God would be the judge of beauty and not the artist.

I must have looked at the rough photocopy of *The Great Piece of Turf* pinned to the office wall hundreds of times over the last few years, and I am wondering now if the original is included in the exhibition at the National Gallery. I expect to find out very soon – if I ever get there.

I cross over the road to take a short cut through the grounds of St Thomas' Hospital, hurrying onto the walkway beside the river where two people in fluorescent orange jackets are planting a tree further back along the path. I can't work out what it is, they are too far away. But it is good to see anyway, maybe an oak or a willow for the embankment.

The time has run out and I am still the wrong side of the river, but the Thames takes no interest in me or my troubles and just rolls on as ever. Dashing over Westminster Bridge, I head towards Whitehall and run up the steady incline, being careful not to collide with any other pedestrians, although luckily there are not many around.

By now I am properly late. Rose will be waiting on the steps unsure what has happened – she might be wondering if we have missed our appointed time and won't be allowed to go into the gallery at all.

The air on Whitehall is poor and I can taste the pollution from the traffic. My eyes are moving much faster now, trying to take everything in. I have now broken into a full run, going as quickly as I can and breathing hard as a hundred disconnected things crowd into my mind all at once.

The top of the road appears at last and there is suddenly so much traffic. Without thinking, I step out to cross and almost walk right in front of a huge double-decker bus. The driver brakes hard and presses his blaring horn, catching my eye as he wearily shakes his head in disapproval. Then a moment later, I am walking across the wide-open spaces of Trafalgar Square, quickly past the lions cast in bronze, past the fountains cascading into their pale blue pools of clean water.

Once there were real lions roaming around these parts, as well as hippopotamus, straight-tusked elephants and woolly mammoths. But all of that was at least 120,000 years ago, when there were lakes and watering holes here instead of all this glass and concrete. The evidence of these long-disappeared creatures' presence comes from the many fossil remains that have been uncovered by human excavations, mostly found in the 1800s, perhaps connected to the construction of Nelson's Column or the first digging works to build what eventually became the London Underground system.

Those fossils are now catalogued and stored in the Natural History Museum.

Nearing the National Gallery, I stumble slightly as I go, although there is nothing to trip over on the stone steps. Rose has arrived already. I can see her waiting near the main doorway, although she has not seen me yet. Slowing down and then slowing down even more, I would like to appear a figure of natural calm as I arrive. My feet are hardly moving now, like one of those dreams where the dreamer is running and running but not getting anywhere. It is only a few more yards and then we will both be through that door and in the high-ceilinged hallways of the gallery and away from the noise and hubbub of Trafalgar Square.

Once in there, everything will slow down, time will change again and move in a different way when we are surrounded by all the paintings and statues. Galleries and museums can be places outside the regular measures and confines of time. Gardens can be as well; you can lose track of the hours and it is only the differences in light and temperature that give indications of the day passing. The trees and plants and all the wild creatures have their own sense of it, their own idea of the various cycles they are following. It is different to us, I think, far more different than we ever realise. Somehow, nothing ever comes to an end. It all seems to be cycles that reach a point of change and then begin again in a new way.

Onwards we go, into the first room of the exhibition to look at the first pictures arranged on the newly painted walls. The light is soft and the air is hushed. Thankfully, my heartbeat has slowed. I am breathing calmly and quietly so nobody would even guess at all the running and stumbling I have done to get here.

MYCELIUM UNDERGROUND

February is nearly over and things are beginning to look a little brighter. Spring will not be long now, only a week or two away, and the first flowers of the year are making an appearance. Early snowdrops are flowering all around the garden.

Being so widespread in England, snowdrops are often described as English natives but apparently that is inaccurate, given that they were introduced from mainland Europe at some point in the 1500s. In horticulture, a British native is described as a plant that was present here during the last ice age, a time that came to an end around 11,000 years ago. By that definition, five centuries of snowdrops being quietly present every spring is not enough for them to be considered indigenous to this country. Whatever the case, their flowers are a warming sight on a February day, whether in a garden or a wilder woodland.

Traditionally, parts of the plant have been used as a treatment for headaches but more recently modern science has been exploring a lectin in snowdrops called GNA with the hope that it might have a potential use in combatting HIV. There is also a compound in the bulb that is being used to treat dementia.

This morning, the lawns at Lambeth Palace are covered with a layer of frost. The stone steps are slippery and there are pockets of ice showing in the flower beds. Then the sun comes out, without warning, through a gap in the heavy grey clouds; the rays are low enough at this time of year to find an angle that catches some of the snowdrop flowers by surprise as if switching them on with the sudden light. Thousands of them, caught meandering through the garden and glorious to see, especially for anyone lucky enough to be out here so early in the day.

To a snowdrop expert, probably every single specimen in this garden would be classed as common. There are so many different variations and new species continue to be discovered every year. Specialist collectors around the world have been known to pay hundreds of pounds for a rarity. While working in Devon, I met someone who kept a camera trained at all times on their snowdrop collection for fear that another collector might make an unannounced visit, appearing in an unmarked van and making off with pots full of especially valuable rare plants.

It is understandable that someone might feel that way, but I could never go so far. I couldn't be the thief with the van in the night nor the watchful guardian trying to safeguard the plant collection. One of the good things for me in horticulture is the sharing of what each gardener has got, so if I have something good or maybe just interesting, I generally want others to have the chance to enjoy it as well. There is no way to count the times I have been given free gifts of plants and plant material by fellow gardeners, and I have tried to do the same in return whenever I can.

Most of the snowdrops in the garden are growing in light shade under deciduous trees, which is their preferred location. Looking closer, I can see there are tiny white bulbils scattered everywhere on the dark surface of the soil, a little green shoot emerging from some of them as the plant tries to grow, even though no part of it is anchored to the ground. If I gently push each of the miniature bulbs with the tip of my finger into the ground, maybe they will have a better chance to mature and come to something next year.

I might be feeling the cold this morning, but there are still a few bees moving around and checking the garden. Some are visiting the little white bells of these flowers at my feet, although the flowers themselves do not require pollination as they will set seed anyway. Sometimes, ants gather up those seeds and, on the way back to the nest, they eat the parts of the coating that are rich in oil and then discard the rest, so helping distribute the seeds still further.

Snowdrops usually spread by growing into clumps that steadily increase in size, making many offsets that can go on to form new plants. When the flowers are finished on these ones I am looking at now, with a fork I will slowly ease out some of the bigger clumps, divide them up and plant them in suitable areas that do not have any snowdrops yet.

This tendency to move plants and try them out in different places is something that runs deep in the history of gardening. For many centuries, plants have been transported from one country to another, sometimes crossing and re-crossing oceans and continents.

In the case of these snowdrops, I am only going to move them a short distance when the time comes, hopefully providing them with a helping hand to do what they want to do anyway, which is to get around and about the place as much as possible. Eventually, the whole garden could be a mass of them each February, quickly fading by March as the green leaves die down, only to start all over again the following year.

Now the sun has gone, with its morning rays hardly having touched the frost on the grass. Maybe I should return to the shed and get warm, making sure to avoid the frozen puddles in the tarmac near the buildings. On my way, I pass by the old quince tree and see how much smaller it seems in February now the branches are bare of leaves. Every year I have been here, this quince has been weighed down with hundreds of yellow fruits. Sadly, not last summer; a few ripened but not nearly as many as usual. There were plenty of flowers, but for some reason they were not properly pollinated. Maybe there were not many insects flying due to the strange weather all through last May.

When holding Garden Open Days for local charities, the garden team would arrange a stall in the entranceway with various spare plants for sale, as well as any produce that was not needed, including the fruit from the quince tree. These went for just £1 each, a fair price I would have said, although several of the visitors coming in told us they had seen quinces on sale for £4 each at Waitrose, a mile down the river by Vauxhall Station. The pressure of market forces, I suppose – they know the margins and they know what they are doing down in Vauxhall.

All of that seems a long time ago. Standing by the tree now, I am looking at the grass growing thinly underneath and, sure enough, a few snowdrops have even made their way to flower there. But I have not forgotten about the pink pyramidal orchid that appeared under this quince tree for the first time last spring. I wonder if it will come up again. And if it does, I wonder if it will be alone, like before, or if maybe it was visited by butterflies and moths, allowing it to set seed so that a few more orchids might show up later this year. I will have to wait a few more months to see.

This type of wild orchid must form an association with various specific fungi in the soil to grow successfully; perhaps a fungus such as fusarium. Together, they form a symbiotic association that is described as a mycorrhizal relationship.

More than twenty years ago, part of my role when working for the National Trust was to help organise training for the garden staff in the Devon and Cornwall region. The gardeners would suggest subjects and I would try to find people to come and talk to us, to show and explain to us modern gardening techniques and practices in depth, especially where ideas were changing. We would meet up for these training days in the most appropriate National Trust property we could find. There were sessions on all kinds of things, ferns, lichens, garden invertebrates, how to look after ponds and lakes, how to manage a meadow. We even spent a day looking at the rich plant life of Cotehele in Cornwall with Roy Lancaster, a gardening legend and an inspiration to so many of us gardeners.

I remember conversations with Roy's great friend Michael Hickson when he was head gardener at Knightshayes in Devon. I remember once when I was visiting, he suggested something for one of our training days. 'Gardeners don't know enough about mycorrhiza,' he said, with a smile.

'Ah, yes indeed. Mycorrhiza, it's true we don't know enough,' I replied, realising that although I had gathered something about it along the way, it wasn't that much and perhaps I was exactly one of those gardeners he was referring to, one of those who didn't know enough.

Via mycorrhiza, plants connect to the underground network of mycelium, which allows the plant to extend the spread of its roots potentially by many miles, offering possibilities for a much increased uptake of water and dissolved nutrients. It is reckoned that more than 90 per cent of plants are reliant on this process. As Michael said, an understanding of mycorrhiza is necessary for all gardeners. So, a training day was organised and about twenty of us gathered from various different gardens. We found our way to a little church hall somewhere in Cornwall on a stormy morning as cold as this one in London but with a wild Cornish gale blustering outside.

There were several talks. One person gave a presentation with some aerial images of a major road system that had recently been built somewhere nearby, possibly something to do with improving access to the Eden Project, which was still quite a new thing back then. The pictures showed where normal road construction practices had taken place with little concern for the soil, where the ground had been excavated with heavy machinery and compacted. Those were contrasted with other examples of roadside verges in different parts of the same site where a management plan had been put in place that required more special care; where some attempts were made to protect the soil structure and the mycelium within it, incorporating additional mycorrhizal fungi with the hope it would attach to the plant roots and help those new plants to establish and grow.

This second way of working was more expensive and more time-consuming as it involved disturbing the ground as little as possible, which meant that everything took longer to do. We were shown images taken from the air a year later. The first series of these showed the poor and stunted growth of the plants put in at the roadside in the areas that had been run as a typical building site. Many of the plants looked in a woebegone state and most appeared to be dead or dying.

Then we saw the other areas where soil disturbance had been kept to a minimum and mycorrhizal fungi had been added. The same range of plants had been chosen as for the other parts of the site but in the photographs we could see that the plantings were thriving and already looked quite well established, even after such a short time. Although the initial cost may have been more, the building contractors explained to us that they had made significant savings in the longer run as they would not have to keep restocking the areas, given there were far fewer plant failures.

There was a break in our training day for sandwiches, drinks and maybe a biscuit. A burst of hail fell like scattershot from above, firing down on the thin roof over our heads as the church hall windows rattled in their old wooden frames, shaken by a wind that howled briefly and then subsided. I sat there wondering about my own garden, faraway over the border in Devon, wondering if the same storm was coming in off the sea to cause havoc among the trees. I would find out soon enough when I got back there.

In the afternoon, another speaker gave us a more general insight into the world of mycelium, explaining that it covered most of the earth. It grew, mostly hidden from us, below the surface and even under the oceans. He said that if it were somehow possible to take an X-ray of the planet, we would be able to see it for ourselves and maybe get a glimpse of how vast this network of branching hyphae is with the countless phantom threads of mycelium down there linked together, branching and re-branching as they move in every possible direction.

Life on earth would not be possible without this mycelia. They are everywhere, supporting all kinds of life forms, including the biggest living organisms and some of the smallest. We know of around 391,000 plant species that flourish on our planet but there are estimated to be over 3.8 million different types of fungi that have been identified so far, with more and more being discovered each year.

There is so much that is still unknown and research into mycelium continues. One especially fascinating piece of ongoing recent research has found evidence that trees make use of the mycelium network as pathways for communication between each other, sometimes diverting extra nutrition via the fungal threads to provide support to others of their species that might be weaker or struggling. This help can give those trees or seedlings improved chances of surviving the attacks of pests or disease, coping with extreme weather and other possible threats.

The plants around us take in carbon dioxide and exchange that for oxygen. Some of the carbon is stored in the leaves, stems and branches but around 70 per cent of it goes below ground, where the plant root systems exchange it with the mycelium network for nutrients, the carbon being deposited to stabilise in the cell walls of the attached mycelium.

Fungi are also essential to the planet's lifeforms as they cause organic compounds to decompose, making room to allow new life in the space to become established. In the garden, thinking about decay cannot be avoided. It is an integral part of gardening, with the cycles of decay and regeneration at constant work through all the seasons. Soon the spring will come to the garden where I am standing now, bringing a tremendous surge of energy to return vibrant green life to all those plants around me that appear dead on this winter day.

The same vital energy surge is felt each year by the trees all around us. They dropped their leaves through the autumn to let them rot on the ground but in the spring they will start all over again when they sense the days are lengthening and the weather is warming up. Linking all these organic activities, driving the rhythm of decay and regeneration, is the mycelium network everywhere beneath our feet. It is a living organism as old as life on earth.

I am walking slowly back along the gravel path towards the compost heaps thinking about those cycles of decay and renewal. Often these compost sites where the garden green waste is recycled tend to be hidden away in a distant corner and made as invisible as possible. But they should be a main attraction in any garden. They are the power station that keeps the garden alive and healthy, the place where rotting matter can be found teeming with earthworms and so much other life.

SPRING COMES AGAIN

M arch and April are the months full of the early flowers, the months full of promise. In the lawn this morning, the first new daisies are beginning to show, joined by buttercups that shine bright yellow against the mossy grass.

There are clusters of goldfinches darting around, filling the air with their thin silvery songs, singing so high their notes seem to shimmer. They are one of the smallest birds to visit an English garden and not a rare sight, although I don't remember seeing them in central London before. Their diet is mostly insects, sometimes feeding on aphids and small spiders, maybe moth eggs as well. Yesterday, I saw them gathered in small groups at the foot of the big cedar tree seeming to be taking an interest in some clumps of dandelions growing there. The birds must have found some bugs to feed on in the dry shelter of the cedar's fallen needles.

The goldfinches flew away as I passed by too near, so I went to take a look at the dandelions under the tree. The word comes from mispronounced French, *dent de lion*, or lion's tooth, as the foliage is thought to resemble the shape of teeth. Those wild plants are beginning to come into flower, and before long, their blooms will be like small yellow suns, turning to pale moons as they ripen into soft globes of seed. These will disperse when ripe, each seed with its own little parachute as they drift on the breeze. Some seeds will travel as far as 60 miles before finding a suitable place to land and germinate.

Earlier on, as I walked across the main courtyard, the sight of the four magnolias around the central monument stopped me in my tracks for a few moments, covered as they are just now with cups of pale pink flowers. Those blooms do not last for long but the trees are having a good beginning to their year.

Moving on through the archway and into the main garden, I find more pink, this time flower petals from a big ornamental cherry by the gate swirling gently down in a soft pink storm. Standing there on the path with the garden opening up before me, there is something different in the air and it feels as if the long winter is over at last. The days are slowly getting longer and everything seems ready to begin again.

I hesitate for a few moments, thinking about nothing very much, when something flies towards me, small and moving quickly in zigzags. It is a sulphur-coloured brimstone butterfly swerving past, the first of the year breaking out and taking wing after months spent quietly overwintering safely in a hidden corner.

Butterflies have compound eyes made of many lenses and, therefore, can see many things in different directions at the same time. Those eyes may not see as sharply as a human eye but they are better at detecting fast movement and can perceive a wider range of colours, including ultra-violet, which helps them identify the species and gender of other butterflies they might notice on their travels. The brimstone flew by and fluttered rapidly away.

By the afternoon, a few other butterflies had put in an appearance, two perfect small tortoiseshells on the viburnum as well as a speckled wood settling on the wood chip path further down the garden. It is only mid-March but the thermometer has reached 25 degrees already today. I hope those butterflies have not come out too early. The temperatures are forecast to descend close to zero again next week. But, at least for a while, the sun is shining and there is colour everywhere. I can see hellebores in all the shades of pink, purple and green, blue chionodoxas and yellow aconites, along with anemones and daffodils, epimediums and others. It goes on and on. The closer I look, the more I find.

Flowering plants first began to appear on Earth around 100 million years ago, according to the evidence of fossil records, and their very rapid evolution from that time has been a puzzle to science for centuries. Charles Darwin referred to this phenomenon as 'the abominable mystery' and even feared that the inexplicable speed with which flowering plants spread and diversified could undermine some of his theories regarding evolution. He pondered how it could have happened so quickly in comparison to the way other life forms changed and evolved.

The much older plant types, such as ferns and conifers, were around more for more than 250 million years before the first flowers appeared and despite having had so much more time on the planet, they are nowhere near as diverse. Conifers and cycads are estimated at about 1,000 species and ferns at 1,300, compared with at least 370,000 species of flowering plants.

There are only a few conifers in the garden at Lambeth Palace; a couple of umbrella pines in the orchard area and then, in the main garden, the big cedar tree where I saw the goldfinches with the dandelions. A few years ago, I planted three cryptomeria conifers nearby to keep the cedar company. They are elegant trees with soft foliage that changes colour in different seasons, following the changes in the weather, going from feathery green to deep oranges and reds as the days turn colder, then sprouting fresh green leaves when spring comes again.

Although the wildlife is active all around, somehow the garden still feels rather big and empty with hardly any people wandering the paths or resting on the benches. Looking at the high walls that surround us here, I realise they were built in the first place to keep the rest of the world out, but I wonder now if they are also keeping everything here closed up and perhaps too much apart. It has been good to see the NHS staff in the garden from time to time. We see very few other people but maybe one day, it will be possible to open the gates more often and let more visitors come in to experience what is here for themselves. If it were up to me, that is what I would try to do, open the gates whenever I could, even if it were only for a few hours on particular days. The entrance charge could be kept fairly low, maybe just enough to cover costs. Or perhaps there would be no charge at all, the entrance could be free.

Meanwhile, with binoculars, I stand here on my imaginary veranda, looking out at the spring garden, some of which may also be imaginary. The cat is asleep on a cushion in the corner. These are mornings filled with small things and I am thankful for that, for the simple pleasures that come and go. I am glad for those moments, even if they are fleeting.

I have been dreaming of the brimstone and the goldfinch, the sage and the salvia, the olive and the fig. But now I must put all of that to one side. I have to gather up my gardening things and get going. There is so much to do.